TREASURES FROM PAUL'S LETTERS

VOL. I

by

Anthony M. Coniaris

Sermons on the Sunday Epistle lessons as read in the Eastern Orthodox Church. Volume I covers the months of September through February.

Z
FOS
E

Light and Life Publishing Company
P.O. Box 26421
Minneapolis, Minnesota 55426

Library of Congress Catalog Card No. 78-56638

TABLE OF CONTENTS

No Other Foundation

Ninth Sunday of Matthew (I Corinthians 3:9-17)

The Imperial Hotel in Tokyo was built to withstand shattering earth tremors in a land of earthquakes and tidal waves. The architect discovered that eight feet below the surface lay a sixty-foot deep bed of soft mud. The idea came to him to float this great structure on the bed of mud which would act as a shock absorber of the earthquakes.

He was ridiculed by many but when the worst earthquake in 52 years struck Tokyo, other well-built buildings collapsed but the Imperial Hotel stood firm and unshaken. It was all in the foundation.

In the Epistle lesson today St. Paul speaks of various foundations on which people build their lives: gold, silver, precious stones, wood, hay, stubble. He speaks also of a Day on which it will be revealed on what kind of foundation each person has built his life. Some foundations will survive, he says; others will not. Then he says, "Let each man take care how he builds . . . For no other foundation can anyone lay than that which is laid, which is Christ Jesus."

Everyone of us is building a house called life. It is a lifetime job. Everything we think and do and say goes into the structure to become part of our life house. One day—said Jesus—this life house will be tested to see of what material it is made. The storm will come. And whether the house stands or falls will be due not to the weather but to the stuff that went into it, to the foundations underneath.

The following story illustrates the importance of a solid foundation in life. A husband was trying to hang a picture on the living room wall. Even though he was standing on a chair, he could not quite reach the desired spot. His wife placed a small wobbly stool above the chair for additional height. Stepping on the stool and balancing himself precariously, the husband gave the nail a few cautious, almost gentle taps with his hammer. The wife then asked in a peevish tone, "Why don't you give it a hard blow or two to get it in?"

Looking down from the wobbly stool on top of the kitchen chair, the husband replied to his wife, "How can a man strike a solid blow when he is standing on a foundation like this?"

The Shaking of the Foundations

How can a person do anything, and do it well, if he stands on a wobbly foundation? Paul Tillich, the famous theologian, wrote a book called "The Shaking of the Foundations." His thesis is that the foundations of the earth are shaking today. Science has unlocked the secret power of the universe. It not only has the power to shake the foundations of the earth; it has the power to destroy earth itself.

A missionary in Africa whose wife died was sent home on furlough. Together with his small son he set out. First by wagon over bumpy roads, then by ocean steamer. Rough weather was encountered on the ocean, and the boat began to pitch and roll. Frightened by all this, the boy turned to his dad and said, "Daddy, when will we have a home that won't shake?"

Wobbly foundations! Shaking foundations! Not only those of the earth on which we live but also those on which we build our lives. But always there comes a day of testing. Always there comes a day of crisis to test the foundation on which we have built our life. Jesus described it when He spoke of the house which had been built on a solid rock, "And the rain descended, and the floods came, and the winds blew, and beat upon that house; and it fell not." For it had been founded on a rock.

A Foundation That Holds

A foundation that holds; a foundation that does not shake; a foundation that affords security in time of need, that solid foundation is none other than Christ. "For no other foundation can anyone lay than that which is laid, which is Christ Jesus." "He who hears my words and does them builds his life on a solid rock," said Jesus. Christ is the foundation on which all foundations are laid; the foundation that cannot be shaken, immovable, unchangeable, unshakable, eternal. The earth may crumble but the rock of our salvation remains unmoved. "Give me a place on which to stand," said Archimedes, "and I can move the earth." Such a standing place is Christ.

A story is told of a little boy who fell out of a boat and climbed upon a rock during a storm. After he was rescued, he was asked if he had been afraid. "Sure, I was afraid," he replied, "I trembled all over, but never once did the rock ever tremble."

Said the Psalmist: "The Lord is my rock, and my fortress, and my deliverer, my God in whom I take refuge, my shield, and the horn of my salvation, my stronghold" (Psalm 18:2).

Are you building your life on this rock?

Jesus called Peter a Rock. It is on such believing, fully surrendered persons that Jesus has built His Church through the centuries. "You are Peter—a rock, and upon this rock I will build my church." Peter's faith made him a rock.

Facing the Test

One winter night a fine old Scotsman lay dying. The wind howled through the trees and blew the peat smoke into the room. The rain lashed at the windows. It was a wild night.

Only his daughter and he were in the house. Realizing that the end was approaching, the daughter turned to him and said, "Father, would you like me to read the Bible to you?" "No, lassie," said the old saint, his eyes full of the light already streaming in from the other land, "I thatched my house before the storm began." His house had been anchored on the Rock. It was withstanding the storm. "Let each man take care how he builds. . . . For no other foundation can anyone lay than that which is laid, which is Christ Jesus."

Not a Sham Rock

A street preacher in London many years ago was preaching to a crowd that had gathered around him. It was the time of the Shamrock Races, and everyone was talking about the event. A ruffian on the edge of the crowd, desiring to have a little fun, called out, "Mr. Preacher! What do you know about the Shamrock?" The preacher continued his preaching. A second time the heckler called out, "I say, Mr. Preacher, what do you know about the Shamrock?" Still the preacher paid no attention. Finally, not meaning to be silenced, he called out a third time, "Mr. Preacher! I'm asking you what you know about the Shamrock!" This time the preacher paused. The crowd became very still. Pointing upward with one hand, he said, so clearly and distinctly that all could hear him, "On Christ the Solid Rock I stand; all other rocks are—sham rocks!"

"Let each man take care how he builds . . . For no other foundation can anyone lay than that which is laid, which is Christ Jesus."

Are You an Actor or a Reactor?

The Tenth Sunday of Matthew (I Corinthians 4:9-16)

"When reviled, we bless; when persecuted, we endure; when slandered, we try to conciliate. . . ." (I Cor. 4:16)

A man once bought a paper from a newsboy. He greeted the boy very courteously. The response was highly discourteous. The paper was shoved rudely in his direction. Whereupon the purchaser politely smiled at the boy and wished him a happy weekend.

Observing this behavior, a friend commented to the person who was kind in the face of such rude behavior, "Why are you so polite to him?" The answer he received was, "Why not? Why should I let *him* decide how *I'm* going to act?"

The most important word here is the word "act." The newspaper purchaser *acted* toward people while most of us *react* toward them. He was his own person. He did not let others determine his behavior. He was free. He was not at the mercy of all the meanness, impatience, pettiness and anger of others. He was in command. He was not controlled by other people's principles but by his own. He did not say what we so often say, "He made me so angry. The very sight of him makes me boil. He really got to me." Instead of allowing the atmosphere around him to transform him, he acted to transform the environment around him.

Who Determines Our Behavior

Most of us are like people attending a live TV show. When the prompter lifts the sign "applause," they all applaud. When the sign "laughter" is raised, they all laugh. Many of us are like slaves meekly reacting when we are told to react. We let someone else's signals determine how we are going to act.

We are not in command. We are not our own persons. We are *reactors* rather than *actors.* We wait to see how others will act toward us before we decide how we will act toward them. If they are kind, we will be kind. If they ignore us, we will ignore them. If they praise us, we will praise them. If they criticize us, we will criticize them. How miserable not to be in command; to be constantly at the mercy of another person's whims; to let others live our lives.

Sometimes we recognize that *reacting* this way is sick behavior. This is why a good psychologist will ask a person in trouble, "*Whom* are you acting *against? Whom* are you getting drunk *against? Whom* are you committing adultery *against? Whom* are you rebelling *against?" Reacting* is at the basis of much of the anti-social behavior in our world today.

An actor does not let others decide how he is going to feel today; whether he is going to be happy or unhappy, polite or rude, irritable or calm. He decides himself how he is going to feel, and he does not let others sidetrack him. He knows that when he takes the initiative to be kind and friendly toward others, most of them will return it—and if they do not, they are the ones who have a problem.

God Does Not React

God is an actor not a reactor. When we sinned against Him and ran off to hide from Him in the Garden of Eden, God did not remove Himself from us. When Adam hid among the trees, God went after him in love, "Adam, where are you? . . . Come let us reason together. Though your sins be as scarlet, they shall be made white as snow."

Jesus had much to say about *reactors*. "If you love those who love you, what credit is that to you? For even sinners love those who love them. And if you do good to those who do good to you, what credit is that to you? For even sinners do the same. And if you lend to those from whom you hope to receive, what credit is that to you? Even sinners lend to sinners, to receive as much again" (St. Luke 6:32-34). These are the reactors who give love for love, kindness for kindness, loan for loan. That's not what true love is all about, says Jesus. He goes on immediately calling on us to be *actors*: "But love your enemies, and do good, and lend, expecting nothing in return; and your reward will be great, and you will be sons of the Most High; for he is kind to the ungrateful and the selfish. Be merciful as your Father is merciful" (St. Luke 6:35-36). Be an actor, like God. Treat hatred with love. Overcome evil with good.

Those who hate us do not win until we hate them back. If we do, then that hatred destroys us. This is why we are called to respond to hatred with the love of Christ.

St. Paul writes in the Epistle lesson today, "When reviled (we do not revile in return), we bless; when persecuted (we do not persecute in return), we endure; when slandered (we do not slander), we try to conciliate" (I Corinthians 4:13). Actors, not reactors!

When Jesus was treated so unjustly, He did not react; He acted. He prayed, "Father, forgive them, for they know not what they do."

None of us is responsible for all the things that happen to us, but all of us are responsible for the way we act when they do happen; whether we act or react. What happens around us is largely outside our control, but the way we choose to respond to what happens is inside our control.

The committed Christian does not let the behavior of others determine how he is going to act or feel. He is in control. He decides. This is because his life is controlled by Christ. "It is no longer I who live, but Christ who lives in me:

and the life I now live in the flesh I live by faith in the Son of God, who loved me and gave himself for me." It is not the behavior of others but "the love of Christ" that controls us, says St. Paul (II Corinthians 5:14).

Living Examples

Let me conclude with a few examples.

Perulia Leprosarium was set up by German missionaries whose child caught leprosy in India and died there of the dread disease. Instead of reacting and saying, "Why did this happen to us?" they acted, controlled by the love of Christ. They said, "Well, since our child has been taken by leprosy, we will establish a leprosarium for others afflicted with leprosy." Tens of thousands of patients have gone through that leprosarium because of the missionaries who took calamity and turned it into opportunity in the name of Christ. Actors, not reactors!

In Fuchow, China, there are three graves side by side. Two of them are the graves of sisters who went out from Australia as missionaries to China, and were murdered. When the news reached their sixty-two year old widowed mother she sold all she had and travelled to the very place where her girls had been killed. She learned Chinese, opened a school, and gave twenty years' devoted service to the people of that land. When she died she was buried beside her daughters. She was an actor, not a reactor!

One day as Dr. Carver, famous black scientist and professor, passed a big house, a woman called to him: "Hey, I need some wood cut." Dr. Carver took off his coat and went about cutting the wood. He carried a load of it into the kitchen, then picked up his coat and went on his way. After he had gone, a servant said to the woman, "That was Professor Carver."

Horrified that she had treated the famous professor so badly, the woman went to the university to apologize. Dr.

Carver smiled and said, "That's all right. I like to do things for my friends." He was an actor, not a reactor!

If you shake a cup that is filled, what spills out but that which is in it? When we are shaken by the problems and pains of life, what spills out of us should be the Christ Who is in us: His love, His peace, His patience, His joy, His power. For our personhood depends not on who or what is around us, but on Who is within us: Christ.

So, "When reviled, we bless; when persecuted, we endure; when slandered, we try to conciliate . . ." (I Cor. 4:16). With God's grace we become actors instead of reactors.

"And Last of All He Appeared Unto Me Also"

12th Sunday of Matthew (I Corinthians 15:8)

" . . . he appeared to Cephas, then to the twelve. Then he appeared to more than five hundred brethren at one time, most of whom are still alive, though some have fallen asleep. Then he appeared to James, then to all the apostles. Last of all, as to one untimely born, he appeared also to me" (I Corinthians 15:5-8).

Christ is risen!

How do you know?

There is only one way. Call the witnesses! This was Paul's method. He cites five post-resurrection appearances of Jesus: to Peter, to the twelve, to 500 of the brethren, to all the apostles, and "last of all He appeared unto me also." Paul places Christ's appearance to him on the Damascus Road in the same category with His appearances to Peter, James and the apostles, even though it occurred six years after these appearances. It was a real resurrection experience of the risen Christ. It was the appearance that changed the history of the world; transformed a fanatical persecutor into Christ's greatest friend; gave the New Testament its chief author, and Christianity its greatest teacher, next to Jesus.

"As to One Untimely Born"

Paul says, "Last of all, as to one untimely born, he appeared also to me" (I Corinthians 15:8). Paul did not belong to the original group of disciples. He came after them. Not only that but he felt he was entirely unworthy of such an experience. "For I am the least of the apostles, unfit to be called an apostle, because I persecuted the church of God" (I Corinthians 15:9). Paul never ceased to wonder that God had chosen to reveal Himself to him, the "chief of sinners." He felt it was an act of pure grace and mercy on the part of God. "But by the grace of God I am what I am . . . " (I Corinthians 15:10).

The early Church decreed that no one could be an apostle if he had not personally seen the risen Jesus. An apostle had to be an eye-witness of the resurrection. He had to be able to testify about the facts from direct personal knowledge of Jesus. Paul always insisted that he had this essential qualification: "Am I not free? Am I not an apostle? Have I not seen Jesus our Lord?" (I Cor. 9:1). "Last of all, as to one untimely born, he appeared also to me" (I Cor. 15:8).

His Other Appearances

Following the Resurrection, Jesus appeared to several of His followers at the point of their deepest need.

He appeared to Mary Magdalene in her great grief when she thought her beloved Master was dead. His appearance brought her great joy.

He appeared to Simon Peter in his great sense of sorrow and shame for having denied Jesus. He appeared to assure him that He had indeed been forgiven and accepted.

He appeared to the two travellers on the road to Emmaus who were despairing and doubting, now that their great deliverer had been crucified. His appearance brought them insight and new hope.

He appeared to His disciples in the upper room, hiding behind locked doors for fear of the authorities. His appearance changed those broken men. It made them strong, confident, bold as lions. They sang; they rejoiced; they healed; they taught; they suffered triumphantly—not just for a few days of passing enthusiasm but for the rest of their lives. This miraculous change occurred because Jesus had actually appeared to them.

Jesus Christ is the same yesterday, today, and forever. If He came then, He comes now. If He appeared then, He appears now. If He revealed Himself then, He reveals Himself now. He comes to us now in our sense of grief to comfort us; in our sense of failure and sorrow for sin to forgive us and raise us to our feet; in our periods of doubt and disillusionment to instill new hope; in our sense of fear to uphold us. Jesus is not dead. He is not just a great teacher and a beautiful example. He is the Son of God, the Risen Lord of Glory. He comes today. He appears today to you and me as He did to His apostles, to James, to Cephas, to the 500 brethren, to Paul. "Last of all, as to one untimely born, he appeared also to me."

He Appears Today

In the Matins service of the Orthodox Church the priest takes the Gospel book with the engraving of the resurrected Christ and carries it out to the worshipers for veneration. This beautiful procession represents the risen Lord walking out of His tomb and standing in the midst of His people, as He stood in the midst of His disciples. This liturgical act shows us that Jesus appears to us today. We can touch Him. We can hear Him. We can kiss Him. We can receive power from Him.

"Jesus is not buried in a tomb near Jerusalem. He is living here in my heart. I walk with Him every day." This personal testimony of one Christian can become the testimony of every Christian believer. He comes today!

"He lives!" "How do you know it?" "I know. I just spoke

to Him this morning." He comes through prayer.

After reading a portion of God's word from the Holy Bible, a devout Christian said, "Jesus is real. He seemed to step right out of the Bible to help me." He comes through His written word.

In his drama "The Trial of Jesus," John Masefield portrays a conversation between Longinus, the Roman centurion in charge of the soldiers at the Cross, and Pilate's wife, who asks him, "Do you think He is dead?" "No, lady," replies the centurion, "I don't." "Then where is He?" "Let loose in the world, lady, where neither Roman nor Jew can stop His truth." He comes!

A devout Christian missionary wrote to a friend from his prison cell: "Jesus Christ came into my cell last night, and every stone flashed like a ruby." He comes!

Contemporary Appearances

He appeared to Malcolm Muggeridge, the brilliant and sophisticated British journalist. While in Palestine to film on location the story of Jesus for the B.B.C., he experienced the presence of the living Christ. It was enough to make him forsake his agnosticism and become a fervent Christian. We commend to your reading his book, "Jesus Rediscovered." He comes!

He appeared to Johnny Cash in 1971 to lift him from the hell of drug addiction to a new life in Christ. "I made a complete dedication of my life to Jesus Christ," he said. "I don't have a career anymore. What I have now is a ministry. Everything I have and everything I do is given completely to Jesus Christ." We commend to your reading his biography "The New Johnny Cash"—new because of Christ Who came to him with forgiveness and power.

He appeared to Alexander Solzhenitsyn, Russia's greatest living author and winner of the Nobel Prize for Literature. Born in a Godless state which has used its vast power to crush religion, Solzhenitsyn joined the Russian Orthodox Church in

1971 and received his first Holy Communion. Somehow, during the eight years spent in terrible labor camps, or during his painful bout with cancer, somehow, because he refuses to speak of his conversion, Christ appeared to Solzhenitsyn. He gave him the power to stand up against the might of the Soviet Union and, single-handedly, to expose the horror of the terrible labor camps. On learning that he would receive $80,000 with the Nobel Prize he said he would use the money to build a church in Russia. One of his first acts on reaching Switzerland after being expelled from Russia was to attend the divine liturgy. "Last of all, as to one untimely born, he appeared also to me" (I Cor. 15:8).

Isn't this what really counts? It counted in Paul's life. It counted in the lives of the apostles. Unless He appears to us, all these other appearances that are recorded in the New Testament are just not too real. Every Christian should be able to write a list of the resurrection appearances of Jesus, and then add at the end of the list, as did Paul: "Last of all, as to one untimely born, he appeared also to me."

If He has not appeared to you, He wants to, if you will only invite Him. Never feel you are too great a sinner for Him to come to you. If He came to the "chief of sinners," Paul, He will not hesitate to come to you. He is knocking today at the door to your heart. "Behold, I stand at the door and knock. If any one hears my voice and opens the door, I will come in to him and eat with him, and he with me" (Rev. 3:20). He will appear to you also so that you, too, may be able to say with Paul, "Last of all, as to one untimely born, he appeared also to me" (I Cor. 15:8).

Love with No Strings Attached

Thirteenth Sunday of Matthew

"Let all that you do be done in love" (I Cor. 16:14).

A 7-year-old girl had taken her 4-year-old brother to a birthday party. After awhile, her hostess said, "Your brother surely is a quiet child. He has not moved for thirty minutes." "It's the first time he's worn a necktie," the sister explained. "He thinks he's tied to something."

In today's Epistle lesson St. Paul lays down an important rule of life for all Christians: "Let all that you do be done in love" (I Cor. 16:14).

Since one of the great abuses of love is that it becomes possessive and tries to control, to manipulate, to tie down the person loved, we shall speak today of genuine love which, like the love of Christ, is love with no strings attached.

No Strings Attached

A pastor once tried an experiment with a group of children. He was trying to teach them that God does not attach strings to His love. He handed a bag of suckers to the kindergarten children. But the children noticed a string attached to the bag. Explaining the string, he said, "You probably noticed the string. I attached it to the bag just in case you don't behave. I'll have to take back my suckers if you are not nice in church."

What the pastor did was not as nice as it first seemed. But he wanted to teach the children an important lesson. He wanted them to learn what love is *not*. Love is not possessive, says Paul. It does not tie strings to the one loved.

Jesus does not attach strings to His love for us. He does not say, "I'll love you *if* you behave . . . *if* you are good . . . if . . . if . . . if . . ." This is a conditional kind of love that we often imply to our children. We will love them only if they are good. We will love them only if they get good grades, or if they're on time, or if they will run errands for us. It is as if we are saying to them, "We will not love you when you are bad, or when you have misbehaved, or when you don't deserve to be loved." It is love with strings attached.

Archbishop Anthony Bloom wrote, "Does it not happen all too often that if the victims of our love dared to speak they would plead: 'Oh, please love me less but leave me free. I'm a prisoner of your love; because you love me you want to determine all my life, you want to shape all my happiness. If only you did not love me, I could be myself!' Does that not happen all too often between parents and children, friends, and husbands and wives?"*

It happens when anyone suddenly showers us with gifts, we begin to look for the hidden strings. We see it in the persons who have long-range plans for us and move into our lives with plans for remodeling us—all in the name of love. They want us to respond emotionally to them through manipulation—even quoting scripture to get us to do what they want. They make us feel tied down. Without realizing it, perhaps, most of us attach strings to our love. "I'll love you . . . *if* you love me, *if* you're good, *if* you live up to my expectations."

A person said once, "I had been so hurt by parents who

---

*"Meditations," Anthony Bloom, Published by Dimension Books. Used by permission.

cut me to ribbons that I never learned to give or to receive love. They said they would love me if I got the best marks in school. They would slap me and then say, 'But we love you.' Love based on an 'if' or 'but' is never love. It was a glorious thing to realize that the God of the whole universe loved me, and that His love was not based on anything I did. I didn't have to earn it."

Why Must We Be So Stringy?

Why must we be so full of strings, so anxious to tie people up! This is not the love of Christ! This is not His tender concern! It should make no difference that people do not accept our plans or ideas for them, or do not wave back when we wave to them. We must love them with no strings attached simply because this is the way Jesus loves them, and this is the way He has called us to love them.

This we can do if we will allow Him to fill our lives. He will help us apply His scissors to our many, many strings.

Everyone needs to feel loved for his own personal worth, not for how he acts or looks or for any other reason. Something in us knows that true love is not something earned but something freely given. The only love that works is love with no strings attached. "I love you for yourself . . . just the way you are," are miraculous words. They free a person to be himself, to reach his full potential in Christ.

At the heart of love there is a simple secret: the lover lets the beloved be free. "Love is never possessive. Rather than trying to change the other person, it allows freedom for the other to be uniquely different.

St. Paul says: "Love does not demand its own way. It is not irritable or touchy. It does not hold grudges and will hardly even notice when others do it wrong."

"Him that I love, I wish to be free—even from me," said Anne Morrow Lindbergh. Real love wants the loved one to grow; only counterfeit love wants to tie strings. Real love knows when to leave people alone. It does not impose a mold on other people; it sets us free, allowing us to become what God created us to be.

"Let all that you do be done in love," says Paul. Only let it be like God's love for us in Christ—love with no strings attached.

"Someday," wrote Teilhard de Chardin, "after we have mastered the winds and the waves, the times, and gravity, we will harness for God the energies of love, and then for the second time in the history of the world man will have discovered fire."

PRAYER

Lord, You tied Yourself down to the cross to set us free. When You endowed us with free will, You made sure there were no strings tying us to You. We are not robots, but children. Freely we love You. Freely we serve You. Help us freely to give Your love to others. Amen.

A New Creation

The Sunday Before the Elevation of the Precious Cross

"For neither circumcision counts for anything, nor uncircumcision, but a new creation" (Gal. 6:15).

There is an old fable about a saloonkeeper who sold the old tavern building he had occupied for many years to a local church. The enthusiastic members removed the bar, added some lights, gave the whole place a fresh coat of paint, and installed some pews. Then they opened the doors for weekly services. Because of an oversight, however, a parrot belonging to the saloonkeeper was left behind. On Sunday morning the wise old bird was watching from the rafters. When the minister appeared he squawked, "New proprietor!" As the choir marched in, he quipped, "New floor show!" But when he looked out over the congregation, he was heard to exclaim, "But the same old crowd."

This imaginary tale brings a smile. But when we stop to consider the truth it suggests, perhaps it should move us to tears. It shows that there is hardly a difference between believers and unbelievers, Christians and non-Christians. In fact, it's "the same old crowd."

"What Difference Does It Make?"

An American Bishop who attended a number of church services in Russia was asked by a young girl about the churches in America. After the bishop gave her as complete a picture as he could, she asked him, "But what difference does it make?"

This is the question the world is always asking of us Christians? What difference does Christ make in people? How are you Christians different from others, if you are at all different?

The difference is explained by St. Paul in Galatians 6:15, "For neither circumcision counts for anything, nor uncircumcision, but a new creation." It is not something external on our bodies that sets us apart as Christians. It is something internal, i.e., that through Christ, through baptism, through repentance and the Holy Spirit, we have become a "new creation." As Paul says elsewhere, "If a man is in Christ he becomes a new person altogether—the past is finished and gone, everything has become fresh and new." A new creation! "Behold, I make all things new," said Jesus. A new creation! Christ established the *New* Testament. His people were to be a *new* people who had put off the old Adam and put on the new. "Put off your old nature which belongs to your former manner of life . . . and put on the new nature, created after the likeness of God in true righteousness and holiness" (Eph. 4:22-24). A new creation!

When Columbus returned to Spain he had to prove he had reached another world. His evidence was a new kind of people he had brought back with him—American Indians. The evidence of Christianity, says St. Paul, is a new kind of people, a "new creation."

A New Creation

The Arabs have an old saying: "Tell me that the leopard has changed its spots and I will believe it. Tell me that a man has changed his character and I will not believe it." This is *not* what the Christian religion teaches. The fundamental principle of Christianity is that anyone can be changed in Christ anytime, any place. If he wants to with his whole being, he can become a new creation in Christ.

Paul Tillich wrote, "To sum up the Christian message for our time in two words, I would say with Paul, it is the message of a *new creation.* For the Christ, the Messiah, the selected and anointed one, is he who brings the new state of things."

St. John of the Ladder says, "You will be careful not to condemn sinners if you remember that . . . the thief was one of a band of murderers; but in one moment the miracle of regeneration took place in him." A new creation!

Amazing changes have occurred in science in the past few years. In fact, there have been more changes in the past 40 years than there have been in the past 4000 years. But it seems that in the words of Norman Cousins "man has exalted change in everything but himself."

The Most Needed Change

The most needed change today is in man himself. Unless man changes inside; unless he is born again; unless he replaces selfishness with love, allthe changes of science will be of no avail. Indeed they will only hasten his destruction.

A person once looked at a dinosaur in a museum and said "What happened to them? Why aren't there any dinosaurs living today? What could kill a thing as big as that?"

The guide answered, "Nobody killed them off. They just weren't able to change with their changing environment. When the climate and the environment changed, the conditions were so different they gradually died off."

Man's external environment has changed so much; for example, he has so many weapons of destruction at his disposal that unless he changes within, he may well suffer the fate of the dinosaur.

We may hear some optimistic voices like Carl Sandburg saying, "God made man a changer. He can change himself into a fish and dive deep and stay under water unafraid of any sea animals. He can change into a bird and travel farther with heavier cargo, wider wings, fiercer claws and beaks than any bird. God must have wanted man to be a changer. God wouldn't have put that awful unrest in him."

But the essential change is not for man to change into a bird and fly, but to change the wolf in him into a lamb. This is precisely what man cannot do. This is where he encounters the greatest difficulty. This is the condition St. Paul described as existing in himself: "I do not understand my own actions. For I do not do what I want, but I do the very thing I hate . . . I can will what is right but I cannot do it . . . I delight in the law of God, in my inmost self, but I see my members another law at war with the law of my mind and making me captive to the law of sin which dwells in my members. Wretched man that I am! Who will deliver me from this body of death?" (Rom. 7:15-24).

The trouble, says Paul, is me. I've had more trouble with this self of mine than with anyone else I've ever met. He gets in my way. He drags me down, messes up things for me. He makes a fool of me. The only reason I hang around with him is that I'm stuck with him. I can't get away from him. Wretched man that I am, who will deliver me? This is not only Paul's problem, it is also our problem.

"It's My Character!"

There is an interesting story of a scorpion who, being a very poor swimmer, asked a turtle to carry him on his back across a river. "Are you mad?" exclaimed the turtle. "You'll sting me while I'm swimming and I'll drown."

"My dear turtle," laughed the scorpion, "If I were to sting you, you would drown and I would go down with you. Now where is the logic in that?"

"You're right," cried the turtle. "Hop on!"

The scorpion climbed aboard. Halfway across the river he gave the turtle a mighty sting. As they both sank to the bottom, the turtle said, "Do you mind if I ask you something? You said there'd be no logic in your stinging me. Why did you do it?"

"It has nothing to do with logic," the drowning scorpion replied sadly. "It's just my character."

The One Who Makes All Things New

This is where change is needed: in man's character, in man's nature. Psychiatry has never brought about this change. Neither has psychology or sociology or education or government or communism or socialism or anything else. Only Christ can produce this kind of radical change, so as to make man a "new creation."

He did it for a Former Black Panther leader and radical of the 1960's who returned from exile recently and announced "My life has turned 180 degrees. I have been born again." He did it for a political leader deeply involved in Watergate. He became a new creation in Christ.

Regardless of what your parents or anyone else did to you in the past, you are responsible now to make the right choices to alter your way of life. If you make the choice to let Christ come into your life, to live for Him, you can become a new creation.

"Your self on your own hands is a problem and a pain," said E. S. Jones, "but your self in the hands of God is a possibility and a power." A new creation!

The only one who can recreate us is the One Who created us in the first place. He created us in His own image and likeness. Today He can recreate us in the likeness of His Son and make us partakers of His life.

The author of the Book of Ecclesiastes says, "There is nothing new under the sun." At that time, centuries before Christ came, he could not know the secret. We today know it:

"What's new under the sun?" Life with Christ is new every day.

The Bible is a record not of theories of change but of changed lives. It tells of Jacob the cheater who became Jacob the righteous patriarch of his people. It tells of Moses, the hot-tempered murderer of an Egyptian, who was changed into Moses the patient leader of a chaotic crowd through the wilderness. It tells of unstable Simon who was changed into Peter, the bold herald of the risen Christ. It tells of Saul of Tarsus "breathing out fire and slaughter" against the Christians, who was changed into Paul, the author of the loveliest description of love ever written: "Love bears all things . . . believes all things . . . endures all things. Love never ends." He became a totally new creation in Christ!

The True Ark

Many times the fathers compare the church to Noah's ark. As those who entered the ark were saved from destruction, so those who enter the church today are saved from the universal destruction of sin and death. But the work of the church is higher and more positive than that of Noah's ark. Because under Noah's direction, the ark took in brute animals, and brute animals it released. But the CHURCH, writes St. Chrysostom, under the leadership of Christ, takes sinners and turns them into saints. The cock entered the ark a cock, and a cock he departed. The wolf entered the ark and a wolf he departed. But when someone enters the ark of the church, he enters a cock and departs a dove. He enters a wolf, and departs a sheep. He enters a caterpillar and departs a butterfly. New creations!

The Greatest Art

Longfellow could take a worthless sheet of paper, write a poem on it and make it worth $6000—that's genius!

Rockefeller could sign his name to a piece of paper and

make it worth $1,000,000—that's capital!

Henry Ford could take a piece of metal worth $150 and turn it into a car worth $1500.00—that's skill!

DaVinci could paint a picture on a piece of fifty-cent canvas and make it worth millions—that's artistic ability.

But only Christ can take a soul stained with sin, wash it clean with His precious Blood, put His Spirit within it, and make it a blessing to humanity—that's salvation, that's new creation!

PRAYER

Here I am Lord, make me new. The old is painful. It hurts. I place myself under new management. . Yours. Amen.

You in Me!

"For Me to Live Is Christ"

Sunday following the Elevation of the Precious Cross (Galatians 2:16-18)

There is a story of a monk who knocked on the door of heaven seeking entrance. A voice asked, "Who are you?" The monk replied, "It is I." The door did not open. After many years he tried again. As he knocked the same voice asked, "Who are you?" "It is I," replied the monk. Again, the door remained shut. Finally, he went back. This time he was much older and far wiser as a Christian. When the voice asked, "Who are you?" the monk replied, "You in me," whereupon the voice replied, "Come in."

You in Me.

What is a Christian? Many answers can be given. He is a person who acknowledges that Jesus is the Son of God. He patterns his life after the teachings of Jesus. He has been baptized. He belongs to the Church. He loves his enemies and prays for those who persecute him. He receives the sacraments. He worships every Sunday. He has committed his life to Jesus as God, etc. All these definitions are good, but they are not complete because they have left out the single most important thing about the true Christian: he is one in whom Christ lives. *You in Me*!

St. Paul expressed this when he said, "It is no longer I who live, but Christ who lives in Me . . . " The Lord Jesus expressed it when He said, "I am the Vine, you are the branches. He who lives in Me and I in him, he it is that bears much fruit, for apart from Me you can do nothing" (John 15:5). "He who eats My flesh and drinks my blood lives in Me and I in him" (John 6:56).

You in Me.

The heart of St. Paul's religion is not justification by faith as some think. The heart of Paul's religion is union with Christ. "I live, yet not I, but Christ lives in me"—here is the essence of Christianity. Emmanuel": God with us; "Emmanuel": God *in* us. Paul's favorite expression is the phrase "*in Christ.*" He uses it 164 times in his letters to express the closeness of his union with Christ. We do not speak today of being *in* St. Chrysostom on *in* St. Basil the Great, but we continue to use the phrase *in* Christ. When we do so, we are making a great confession of faith. We are declaring that Jesus is no mere fact of history, no mere towering personality of the past, but the living God present in us now.

You in Me!

Augustine, converted to Christ from a life of complete licentiousness, was walking one day when, across the road, coming in the other direction, appeared one of the many mistreses he had known. She didn't know about his conversion. Beguilingly she called to him. "Augustine!" He went right on his way. She called again, "Augustine! It is I." Augustine, scarcely turning his face said, "Yes, but it is not I!"

Christ was now an indwelling presence—a presence that made all things new! You in Me!

A fellow and a girl were walking along one day discussing a mutual friend. One of them said, "Mary has what I call a radiant personality." "That's right," agreed the other, "but how do you account for it?" Just then they rounded a bend in the road and a rippling river came into view. Pointing to the opposite bank, the fellow said, "See that impressive old castle over there? Well, when I was a small boy, I loved to sit right here in the evening and look at it. I knew what was going on inside by the number of lights that were burning. If only a few people were home, just a faint glimmer filtered through the windows. But when friends came, many lamps were lit and the place became a thing of beauty. One time when a member of the royal family visited there, the entire castle was illuminated! I have never seen such brilliance." Then turning to his companion, he said, "I think that's the only way I am able to explain Mary's shining personality. She is entertaining a Royal Guest!"

We're not castles, but we are temples of the living God. When the Royal Guest is present within, He adds joy and peace and love and light to our lives.

You in Me!

PRAYER

Lord, when I am overlooked, forgotten, or neglected, and my heart continues to be at peace, I know what this is: it is You in me.

When my wishes are crossed, my suggestions are ignored, and my advice is ridiculed, and I continue to be patient and loving,

When I surmount difficulties, when I successfully meet adversity,

When I meet loss, injustice, confusion with poise and serenity, I know what it is: You in me.

When I am content with simple things,

When I return good for evil, when I forgive and turn the other cheek,

When I speak only good of others, see only good in others, I know what it is: You in me!

When I help others, when I go the second mile, when I do more than is expected,

When I speak the word of Truth, when I live the Truth I know,

I know what it is: You in me. Amen.

Claiming God's Promises

First Sunday of Luke (2 Corinthians 7:1)

A famous senator said to his son, "Son, there are two qualities that will get you far in government: integrity and astuteness. By integrity I mean if you ever give your word, keep it. By astuteness, I mean don't ever be dumb enough to give your word."

God both gives His word and keeps it.

A check is a man's promise to pay. It depends entirely upon the signer, his integrity, his word. When you have confidence in a man you take his check as readily as cash. If you need money, you simply endorse it. But refuse to endorse it, and it's useless, so much paper, no matter how much its maker may have in the bank.

The Bible is full of tremendous promises made by God. Back of these promises is God's name, God's integrity, God's tremendous resources. Each one of these promises is for you. They are like checks made out to you bearing God's signature. All that is required is that you have enough faith in the signer to endorse the check (the promise) and cash it.

It is about these promises that St. Paul speaks in the epistle lesson today when he says, "Since we have these promises, beloved, let us cleanse ourselves from every defilement of body and spirit, and make holiness perfect in the fear of God" (2 Cor. 7:1).

A Bank

There are people who think of Christianity in terms of ceremony or ritual or sermons. It strikes them as being dull and not particularly interesting. I like to think of our Christian faith as a bank—God's bank—which offers us countless checks or promises to cover our many needs in life. Many wise Christians, having received these "checks," have cashed them, and continue to cash them daily. As a result they have become rich in personal power and they bless the world by their radiant and useful lives. They never have their "checks" framed to hang them on the wall where they can look at them and imagine how nice it would be to have their prayers answered. They have enough faith in God to take Him at His word.

God's Checkbook

How many Christians, for example, have God's checkbook at home—bound in beautiful leather with gilt-edged pages. They look at the checks once in a while and wish with a sigh that they could be true. Intead of cashing them and claiming the promises, they continue to live on spiritual relief.

Practical Atheists

Thus, it is tragically true that many of us Christians are practical atheists. We profess to believe in God, but we refuse to believe and claim His promises—which is another way of saying that we don't believe in Him. The Lord Jesus makes promises to us such as, "Come to me all you who labor and are heavy laden and I will give you rest," and yet we keep our problems and our worries to ourselves. We don't bring them to Him. We are borne down by them and defeated by them and made anxious by them. He has told us that if we are thirsty in any respect we can come to Him. Whosoever comes to Him will never thirst. Whosoever eats of the bread that He shall give shall never hunger. He has promised to give us "a well of water springing up into everlasting life" so that we shall never thirst. But we do not believe Him. We do not claim the promise. We fail to cash the check. Take all the words and the promises Jesus made when He was here on earth, they are all made for us. They are meant for us today as definitely as when he first uttered them. The trouble is that we do not believe them. It is our "little faith" that stands in the way of receiving His great power.

One Great Claim

There are many fantastic claims being made today by politicians and the advertising industry. The tragedy is that we allow these inflated promises to turn us off to all promises, especially to the *one miraculous claim* which happens to be gloriously true. That Jesus Christ, the eternal Son of God, came down from heaven for you. He suffered for you. He died for you. He was raised from the dead for you, to forgive you, to adopt you, to make you His son or daughter, to fill you with His presence here and now, and to prepare for you a place in the mansions of His Father's house above.

God's Promises for You

When He speaks in the Bible, God is speaking to you. *His promises are for you.*

"Ask and it will be given you. Seek and you will find. Knock and it shall be opened to you." Here is God's promise for you!

"If we confess our sins, God is faithful and just, and will forgive our sins and cleanse us from all unrighteousness." Here is God's promise for you!

"Yea, though I walk through the valley of the shadow of death, I will fear no evil; for Thou art with me. Thy rod and Thy staff they comfort me." God's promise for you!

"Thou wilt keep him in perfect peace whose mind is stayed on Thee" (Isaiah 26:3). God's promise for you!

"You shall receive power after the Holy Spirit comes upon you and you shall be my witnesses" (Acts 1:8). God's promise for you!

"Trust in the Lord with all your heart; and lean not on your own understanding. In all your ways acknowledge Him, and He will direct your path" (Proverbs 3:5-6). God's promise for you!

"We know that in all things God works for the good of those who love Him" (Romans 8:28). God's promise for you!

The statements and the promises God makes in the Bible are for you. They have your name on them. Claim them. Endorse them. Cash them. You were not meant to live in this world as a pauper but as the child of a King.

A Promise Kept

David Livingstone once addressed a group of students at Glasgow University. When he rose to speak he bore on his body the marks of his African struggles. Severe illness on more than thirty occasions had left him gaunt and haggard. His left arm dangled helplessly at his side, the result of mauling by a lion.

He described his bad experiences and said, "I suppose you're going to ask me how I was able to prevail in the midst of all the problems in Africa, with a language I didn't know, with people who were often hostile. I want to tell you. I was able to stay in the jungles in the name of Jesus Christ, for this was my promise from Him—and He kept it—'Lo, I am with you always, even unto the end of the world' " (Matthew 28:20).

God gives His word and keeps it. Do we have enough trust to claim it?

God's Promises: a Savior

All through the Old Testament God keeps promising to send a Savior. He was to come of the family of David. The genealogy of St. Matthew lists the fulfillment of these promises. The sixteen verses (Matthew 1:1-16) show that Jesus was the son of David and the son of Abraham. This was the kingly line from which Christ was to be born. The significance of this is that God keeps His word—His promises are fulfilled.

The promise was that He would be born of a virgin mother. He was!

The promise was that He would be born in Bethlehem of Judea. He was!

The promise was that He would ride into Jerusalem upon a colt. He did!

The promise was that soon after birth He would have to flee into Egypt for safety. He did!

The promise was that when this Messiah came, "the desert would blossom with flowers, the blind would see, the deaf would hear, the lame would walk, and rivers of water would flow in the desert." The promise was fulfilled in Christ!

God revealed to Symeon that he would not die until he had seen the Lord's Christ. Symeon clung to the promise and God honored his heart's desire that day when he saw Mary bringing the Christ child to the temple for the dedication forty days after His birth.

The promise of the angel Gabriel to Mary was that she would bear a great Person: "He will be called the Son of the Most High. He will rule as a king forever. The Holy Spirit will be His Father. He will be called the Son of God. And His name shall be Jesus." God's promise was fulfilled.

God promised through John the Baptist: "Somebody's coming, someone great. Greater than me; greater than any of us; the latch of whose shoe I am unworthy to untie. Watch for this Person and listen to what He says. The kingdom of God is at hand!" The promise was fulfilled.

God promised that this coming Messiah would be "despised and rejected by men; a man of sorrows and acquainted with grief . . . Surely he has borne our griefs and carried our sorrows . . . he was wounded for our transgressions, he was bruised for our iniquities . . . He was oppressed, and he was afflicted, yet he opened not his mouth; like a lamb that is led to the slaughter . . . " (Isaiah 53). This promise was fulfilled on Calvary.

Jesus promised that on the third day He would rise from the dead: "Behold, we are going up to Jerusalem; and the Son of man will be delivered to the chief priests and the scribes, and they will condemn him to death, and deliver him to the Gentiles; and they will mock him, and spit upon him, and scourge him, and kill him; and after three days he will rise." And it came to pass exactly as Jesus promised!

The promise was that on the cross His side would be pierced. It was!

The promise was that He would be betrayed by a friend and sold for thirty pieces of silver. He was!

The promise was that after His resurrection, He would ascend into heaven. He did!

The promise was that after His ascension, the disciples would be filled with the power of the Holy Spirit. They were!

"All the promises of God find their yes, (their fulfillment) in Jesus Christ . . . " says Paul in 2 Corinthians 1:20. God is always true to His promises. He is utterly dependable.

God's R.O.P.

God's R.O.P. (Record of Performance) in the keeping of His promises is spotless. St. Peter speaks about God's flawless R.O.P. when he writes:

"If God did not spare the angels when they sinned, but cast them into hell . . . if He did not spare the ancient world, but preserved Noah, a herald of righteousness, with seven other persons, when He brought a flood upon the world of the ungodly; if by turning the cities of Sodom and Gomorrah to ashes he condemned them to extinction and made them an example to those who were to be ungodly; and if He rescued righteous Lot . . . then the Lord knows how to rescue the godly from trial, and to keep the unrighteous under punishment until the day of judgment" (2 Peter 2:4-10).

Trusting God's record of performance David said as he faced Goliath: "The Lord who delivered me from the lion and the bear, shall he not deliver me out of the hand of the Philistine?" The Lord Who delivered then, shall He not deliver now? He did!

But David had not seen God's Christ on the cross for us. If he had, surely he would have said with St. Paul: "He who did not spare his own Son but gave him up for us all, will he not also give us all things with him?" (Romans 8:32). How can we distrust such a love? How can we disbelieve such a God?

It is always a good exercise to look back and examine God's record of performance. List the many times you waited for something to happen and it happened. Or, if it did not happen, how little it mattered, really. Make a mental list of the blessings the Lord has delivered. They can be endless.

What the Church does in large part is to keep recalling the past to us in order to strengthen us for the present and to give us hope in our waiting. We are reminded of God's care for His people in the past. He created us in love. He chose a people, Israel, to be His instrument of bringing a Savior to all of us. In the fullness of time the Savior came to live and die and rise again for us. God would never have invaded this world in Person if He did not love us and have great plans for us. We do not wait in a vacuum. We wait in the amazing history of a God Who makes and keeps His promises.

The person who feeds his mind and heart on the record of what God has done in the past will never worry about the future. As Fenelon said, "Let gratitude for the past inspire us with trust for the future." Or as Emerson said, "What I have seen teaches me to trust my Creator for what I have not seen."

Even Better Promises

We have mentioned how all the Old Testament promises find their fulfillment in Christ. When Jesus came, it was as if

God said to us: "Here is the One in Whom all my promises come true."

But in Jesus we receive not only the fulfillment of the old promises; we receive also even better promises (Hebrews 8:6; 9:15). Jesus is not only the fulfillment of the hopes and dreams of the past; He brings to us things greater and more precious than we had ever dreamed of.

In other words, Jesus not only fulfills Old Testament promises and ideals; he surpasses them. He brings into life not only something which grew out of the past, but also something that is completely new and surpasses the past.

What are some of these new promises Jesus brought and fulfilled?

THE PROMISE OF THE HOLY SPIRIT: God living in us enabling us to live the life of Christ and do works beyond all our powers.

THE PROMISE OF FORGIVENESS, the restoration of man's broken relationship with God. Through Christ we now become friends of God. When we repent, the Father of the prodigal son waits to embrace us.

THE PROMISE OF ETERNAL LIFE. When we choose to live life with Christ here and now, heaven begins on earth. Into man's trouble and frustration come the peace and power of God.

THE PROMISE OF THE COMING AGAIN OF JESUS. He will come to restore all the imbalances and inequities of life; to establish justice; to destroy evil; to receive His own into His kingdom. The world is not headed toward extinction, toward nothingness, but toward the Second Coming of Jesus.

Listen to this promise for the future:

"Beloved, we are God's children now; it does not yet appear what we shall be, but we know that when he appears, we shall be like him, for we shall see him as he is" (I John 3:2). This is God's promise for the future for God's children. The best is yet to be!

Another promise:

"For I reckon that the sufferings of this present time are not worthy to be compared with the glory which shall be revealed in us" (Romans 8:18). "In the world you have tribulation, but be of good cheer, I have overcome the world." For the Christian the future is as bright as the promises of God.

Condition—Promise

For every promise of God there is a condition. Nowhere did Jesus emphasize this more than in John 15:

"I am the vine, you are the branches. He who abides in me, and I in him, he it is that bears much fruit, for apart from me you can do nothing."

The *promise* is: "Ask whatever you will and it shall be done for you"; the *condition* is: "if you abide in me and my words abide in you" (John 15:7).

The *promise* is salvation; the *condition* is believe in the Lord Jesus.

The *promise* is forgiveness; the *condition* is repent and forsake your sin.

The *promise* is: "Thou shalt keep him in perfect peace"; the *condition* is "whose mind is stayed on Thee."

The *promise* is: "they shall renew their strength, they shall mount up with wings like eagles, they shall run and not be weary, they shall walk and not faint"; the *condition* is "they who wait upon the Lord."

The fulfillment of God's best promises for you depends on one condition: abiding in Christ, living with Him and for Him, surrendering your life completely to Him as Lord and God.

Let me close with two verses from God's word:

"Do not throw away your confidence; it will be richly rewarded. You need to persevere so that when you have done the will of God, you will receive what (God) has promised" (Hebrews 10:35, 36).

" . . . he has granted to us his precious and very great promises, that through these you may escape from the corruption that is in the world . . . and become partakers of the divine nature" (2 Peter 1:4).

"Since we have these promises, beloved, let us cleanse ourselves from every defilement of body and spirit, and make holiness perfect in the fear of God" (2 Cor. 7:1).

PRAYER

Lord Jesus, if all God's promises find their fulfillment in You, I kneel before You today yielding my life completely to You that You may be the fulfillment of God's best promises for me. Amen.

God Loves the Cheerful Giver

Second Sunday of Luke. II Corinthians 9:6-11

Someone wrote, "That money talks,
I do agree;
But it only says
'Goodbye' to me!"

Money talks! But it says more than just "Goodbye!" If a biographer who knew his business wanted to write a book about you, he would want to get his hands on your old checks. They would tell him the truth about the real you. They could tell him, among other things, what kind of person you are. He could find out that you are a member of the church. But suppose that in looking through your checks and other records he learned what your income is, and discovered that in a typical year you spend one per cent of your income for God's work and six per cent for personal luxuries. Would he, or would he not, be justified in saying something like this about you? "On the evidence that we have, it appears that our subject loved the Lord in the amount of one dollar per week, and loved his personal luxuries in the amount of six dollars per week." Money talks! It tells what kind of people we are, what we value most in life, what we love and care for most.

Give Proportionately

A man said to his psychiatrist, "I have one of the most

beautiful homes in Hollywood. I have a chauffeured Cadillac, two swimming pools, a helicopter to take me to the beach club; we belong to an exclusive golf club; I man a yacht with a crew of six, and eat so well my Diner's Club bill averages more than $1,000.00 a month."

"Under those conditions," the psychiatrist said, "what kind of a problem could you have?"

"My problem," said the patient, "is that I make only $50.00 a week." How he lived was way out of proportion to what he earned.

The trouble with most of church giving is that it is out of proportion to what we have, to what we earn. The important thing in Christian giving is not "how much" we give, but "how much in comparison to our ability." A gift does not need to be large in order to be significant. It is great or small in proportion to the amount of other things we possess. One of the greatest examples of Christian stewardwhip is the poor widow who came into the Temple one day and gave "all that she had." It wasn't very much, just a fraction of a cent, but it caused the treasury bell to ring and Christ to give her a commendation that keeps ringing down through the centuries: "Truly, I say to you, this poor widow has put in more than all of those who are contributing to the treasury. For they all contributed out of their abundance; but she out of her poverty has put in everything she had, her whole living" (Mark 12:43, 44).

Give Lovingly

Give proportionately as God has blessed you. And then give *lovingly.* True Christian giving begins with my personal commitment to Christ, and it proceeds from there. It says, "If you don't love God, don't give. God does not need the token support of those who do not really care." And conversely, Christian giving says, "If you do love God, let your giving be some indication of the measure of that love."

Give Generously

Give proportionately, lovingly. Give *generously.* "He who sows sparingly will also reap sparingly." When it comes to giving to God and His work, if you must err, err on the side of generosity, as you would if your loved one were in need and presented a request. Err on the side of going beyond what is practical and try what is spiritual. "He who sows bountifully, will also reap bountifully," writes Paul in the epistle lesson. Give abundatly and you will receive abundantly.

Give Wisely

Give proportionately, lovingly, generously. Give *wisely.* Many of the ancient Greek coins have an owl on them. The owl was there to remind people that they should be as wise as owls in the spending of money. How does a Christian spend money wisely? A wise Christian will sit down and make two columns. Column #1 will be entitled, *"WHAT ARE WE LIVING FOR?"* and Column #2 will be called *"WHAT ARE WE SPENDING FOR?"* For we can never determine wisely what we shall spend for until we realize what we are living for. What we are living for will determine what we do with our possessions.

Give Gladly

Give proportionately, lovingly, generously, wisely. Give *gladly!*"Everyone must give," St. Paul says, "as he has determined in his heart; not grudgingly, nor of necessity, for *God loves a cheerful giver.*" Give from your heart—cheerfully. Even a dog knows the difference between reluctant and cheerful giving. *Throw* him a bone and he'll go away without wagging his tail. But *call* him to you kindly, pat his head, and then give him the bone and he'll go away with a wagging tail. In both cases it is the same act; you gave the bone. It was the spirit of giving that made the difference.

You may remember the farmer's wife who asked her husband as he came in from the barn, "How much milk did the cow give?" He answered grimly, "Nine quarts and a kick." That did it. The kick knocked over the nine quarts and somewhat spoiled the effect of the gift.

An example of cheerful giving is Alvin Dark, former manager of the San Francisco Giants. He wrote,

"Tithing . . . Giving the first tenth of my income back to God was just as unquestioned in our home as putting on my socks before my shoes. And a nickel out of every 50 cents was quite a lot when I got up every day before dawn to pedal around my paper route. But as the years went by and my income increased, I found out I could never win in this game of giving to God. He always outgave me. He gave to me physically, financially and in a dozen other ways. He led me into a satisfying career in baseball. Actually, if I belong to Him, He owns me and my income, too, all of it. I have learned that tithing is just a symbol of my trust in Him."

Give Humbly

Give proportionately, lovingly, generously, wisely, gladly. And finally give *humbly*. Those who follow the Hindu religion must bring their thank offerings to the local priest in the following manner. They fall to their knees, close their eyes, and then place the offering in the open hand of the priest. When asked the reason for this they reply, "We close our eyes because we are ashamed to bring so little. We are ashamed because no matter how great our gift, it is tiny when compared to His love for us. So, as we present our gift, we fall to our knees in deep humility."

How do we give to God? Do we give proportionately? Do we give lovingly, generously, wisely, gladly? Do we give Him not only our money but also our time, our abilities, our talents, even our very lives? No matter how much we give, we ought to close our eyes and fall to our knees humbly because we bring so little when we think of how much He gave for us on the Cross and still gives.

If our giving to God is proportionate, loving, abundant, wise, cheerful and humble, God promises, says Paul "to provide you with every blessing in abundance, so that you may always have enough of everything and may provide in abundance for every good work . . . You will be enriched in every way for great generosity, which through us will produce thanksgiving to God . . ." (2 Cor. 9:8, 11). If our giving is abundant, God's giving to us will be even more abundant.

Do It Anyway

An unknown author wrote these lines entitled "Do It Anyway":

"Some people are unreasonable, illogical and self-centered.

Love them anyway!

If you do good people may accuse you of selfish, ulterior motives.

Do good anyway!

If you are successful, you may win close false friends and true enemies,

Succeed anyway!

The good you do today may be forgotten tomorrow.

Do good anyway!

Honesty makes you vulnerable.

Be honest anyway!

The biggest men with the biggest ideas can be shot down by the smallest men with the smallest minds.

Think big anyway!

What you spend years building may be destroyed overnight.

Build anyway!

People really need help but may attack you if you help them.

Help them anyway!

Give the world the best you have and you may get kicked in the teeth.

Give the world the best you got anyway!"
Give anyway! Love anyway! Help anyway! Build anyway! "He who sows bountifully will also reap bountifully . . . God loves a cheerful giver."

PRAYER

"Lord, Thou didst suffer more for me
Than all the hosts of land and sea.
So let me render back again
This millionth of Thy gift. Amen."
—by Joyce Kilmer

My Weakness—His Strength

Third Sunday of Luke (2 Cor. 11:31—12:9)

"Three times I besought the Lord about this, that it should leave me; but he said to me, 'My grace is sufficient for you, for my power is made perfect in weakness.' I will all the more gladly boast of my weaknesses, that the power of Christ may rest upon me . . . for when I am weak, then I am strong" (2 Cor. 12:8-10).

There is a beautiful story of a sheep that limped and never ventured more than a few feet away from the shepherd. A stranger asked about this sheep—why it limped and why it never left the shepherd's side. The shepherd explained that that particular sheep was born partially deaf and could not hear the shepherd's voice. As a result, it was always walking into danger. Many times it had to be rescued from the brink of destruction. Finally the shepherd had to inflict an injury upon its leg. Since then, the sheep limped, but it also stayed closer to the shepherd for guidance and protection.

Keep in mind this picture of the sheep limping by the shepherd's side and come back to St. Paul in today's epistle lesson. He talks of a similar "limp." He calls it his "thorn in the flesh." It was some chronic illness that caused him great discomfort. To Paul it was "a messenger of Satan, to harass me, to keep me from being too elated. Three times I besought the Lord about this, that it should leave me; but he said to me, 'My grace is sufficient for you, for my power is made perfect in weakness' " (2 Cor. 12:7-9).

The "limp" that afflicted Paul did not come from God. It was, says Paul, "a messenger of Satan." But God did not remove it despite Paul's prayers. His love allowed it to remain in order to keep Paul "limping" at the Shepherd's side where he would find constant strength for his weakness.

When I Am Weak then I Am Strong

When Paul discovered that the true purpose of his thorn in the flesh was to keep him close to the source of power, he gloried in it. "I will all the more gladly boast of my weaknesses, that the power of Christ may rest upon me. For the sake of Christ, then, I am content with weaknesses, insults, hardships, persecutions, and calamities, for when I am weak, then I am strong" (2 Cor. 12:9-10).

When we are weak, then we are strong. When our weakness makes us lean on God's strength, we have more than all the strength of the world. No infirmity can make us infirm if we are firm in the Lord.

Have you ever been driven into a corner from which there seemed to be no way out? If this has happened to you, you may be sure that God allowed it so that He may come with His mighty power to deliver you. But first He wants you to discover that you are powerless and inadequate in yourself and that your dependence must be upon Him. "When I am weak then I am strong."

When We Come To the End of Our Rope

When we come to a place in life where human strength is not enough, we can do one of two things. We can either give up and go down in defeat, or we can find God and move on in His strength.

St. Paul tells of one such experience he had when he says,

"We should like you, our brothers, to know something of what we went through in Asia. At that time we were completely overwhelmed; the burden was more than we could bear; in fact, we told ourselves that this was the end. Yet we believe now that we had this experience of coming to the end of our tether that we might learn to trust, not in ourselves, but in God who can raise the dead." (2 Cor. 1:8-9) God has a purpose in adversity—and that purpose is to make us lean more completely upon his saving arm. "When I am weak then I am strong."

Our real power lies in our powerlessness, in our weakness which makes us cry out to God for help. Then the helpless become omnipotent. Though we are utterly helpless in ourselves, yet we can "do all things through Christ who strengthens" us.

Listen to the Psalmist's experience:

"The cords of death encompassed me,
the torrents of perdition assailed me;
the cords of Sheol entangled me,
the snares of death confronted me.
"In my distress I called upon the Lord;
to my God I cried for help.
From his temple he heard my voice
and my cry to him reached his ears . . .
He bowed the heavens, and came down;
thick darkness was under his feet.
He rode on a cherub, and flew;
he came swiftly upon the wings of the wind . . .
He reached from on high, he took me,
he drew me out of many waters" (Psalm 17).

In his distress the psalmist called out to God, and God "bowed the heavens and came down." His weakness became the place where God's power was demonstrated just as in Paul's life the place of his weakness became the place of God's power. Emerson in his essay on "Compensation" said: "No man had ever a defect that was not somehow made useful to him."

The usefulness Paul saw in his defect was that it drove him closer to Christ. Instead of complaining, he rejoiced in it. Instead of grumbling, he gloried in it. Instead of going on a spree of self-pity, feeling sorry for himself for this trouble that God would not take away, he used it as a stepping stone to power. Can we not also rejoice in whatever God uses to bring us to simple daily dependence on Christ? But we do not merely "glory in our infirmities." We finish the sentence . . . *"that the power of Christ may rest upon me."* That is what matters. We concentrate on His strength, not on our weakness.

A Great Paradox

Here is one of the great paradoxes of the Christian faith: that in weakness there is strength. The wisdom of the world teaches the exact opposite. To be weak, it says, is to be helpless, despised, ineffective. It is to invite the strong to trample upon you. To be weak in education, in marriage, in business is to invite disaster. Only when God enters the picture do things get turned around. It is the wisdom of God that says in Paul, "When I am weak, then I am strong." No casual observer would ever describe Paul as weak. He was one of the most powerful human beings who ever lived. Few people had more vitality, more courage, more endurance, more brilliance of mind than Paul. All of these strengths flowed from his weakness which made him depend completely on Christ. He was one of the faithful described in Hebrews 11, "Who through faith . . . out of weakness was made strong."

So all of the talk we hear about God giving His loved ones a soft ride through this world is totally foreign to the teaching and example of Christ—and to the daily experience of the early church especially as we see it in Paul's life.

Our Emptiness—His Fulness

When we have feelings of weakness or helplessness, let us

not give way to despair. Rather, let us rejoice, for we already have one-half of the necessary condition for receiving power. We have the emptiness to bring in God's fulness. We can link up that emptiness, that inner weakness, with God's power in Christ that we may discover a source of power more than adequate for all our needs. "I will all the more gladly boast of my weaknesses that the power of Christ may rest upon me" (2 Corinthians 12:9).

Acceptance

If we are weak let us admit it and accept it. Let us not pretend to be what we are not—strong. Accept the weakness—but not just the weakness. Accept the fact that such a feeling of inadequacy has come to us only to lead us to Him Who is the real source of all our adequacy, to Him "Who is able to do exceeding abundantly above all that we ask or think." To face our weakness, to accept it, is to find a strength we did not know was there.

Is Religion a Crutch?

An American Christian was traveling in Russia. A Russian woman asked him: "Are you a religious man?" The American replied that he was. She replied, "You are religious because you are weak. You turn to God for comfort. Do you want someone to hold your hand?" She then threw her hand out to the American to show what she meant. The American replied, "I am afraid you are wrong. I don't turn to God for comfort, but for power. I don't want God to hold my hand; I want Him to strengthen my arm so I can give a helping hand to others. I don't want Him to wipe away my tears; I want Him to give me a handkerchief that I might wipe away the tears of others."

When Paul leaned on Christ in his weakness it was not just to receive comfort for himself; it was to enable him to reach out to others with the good news of God's power for our weakness.

Belligerent, a sophomore student said to a college chaplain one day, "Sir, religion is a crutch!" The chaplain replied, "Sure it is. But who isn't limping?" Like the sheep with the broken leg, Paul limped by the Shepherd's side. There he found his greatest strength.

Someone asked Francis of Assisi once how he was able to accomplish so much. He replied, "This may be why: The Lord looked down from heaven and said, 'Where can I find the weakest, littlest man on earth?' The He saw me and said, 'I've found him. I will work through him and he won't be proud of it. He'll see that I'm only using him because of his insignificance.' "

God Chooses the Weak to Shame the Strong

Did not Paul say to the Corinthians, "God chose what is weak in the world to shame the strong . . . so that no human being might boast in the presence of God" (I Corinthians 1:27, 29). It is in weakness that God manifests His power so that the glory might always go to Him.

Lifted From Weakness to Strength

The famous industrialist J. C. Penney tells of the time he had a breakdown. He was in a hospital so depressed that he felt he would die during the night. He wrote farewell letters to his wife and children. "When morning came," he said, "I felt as if the shades had been pulled down, every light extinguished; darkness was all about me. I was utterly without hope. Blackness was in my mind.

"Then from far down the hall I heard singing. They were singing the song, 'God Will Take Care of You.' I listened and suddenly something within me broke: I yielded myself to God. I said to Him, 'Lord, I can do nothing. Please take care of me.' "

After he relinquished himself to God he says, "The darkness ebbed away. It was as if someone had thrown back the curtains and turned on every light in the place. The room was filled with radiance. In my mind, in my heart everything was new. I was happy. I experienced an inflow of power such as I never knew was possible."

He discovered that if a defeated person will realize that he no longer has any power of himself and will yield himself to God in faith he will find a superhuman strength. As two metallic parts become strongest at the point of welding (where they were once weakest), so the power of the risen Christ can make us strongest where once we were weakest.

I Will Gladly Boast of My Weakness

Paul began with a problem, a "thorn in the flesh, a messenger of Satan." He prayed three times, "Lord, take this weakness away from me." God answered him in a way he must have thought strange at first: "You've got a problem? My grace is sufficient for you, for my power is made perfect in weakness." Paul discovered that God was right. In his weakness he leaned on Christ and found power beyond what he thought possible. And this made him say, "I will all the more gladly boast of my weaknesses, that the power of Christ may rest upon me . . . for when I am weak, then I am strong."

PRAYER

O Lord, may our weaknesses and adversities drive us closer to You that we may find in You, as Paul did, the strength to do all things. Amen.

How to Deal With Difficult People

Fourth Sunday of Luke (Titus 3:8-15)

"As for a man who is factious, after admonishing him once or twice, have nothing more to do with him, knowing that such a person is . . . self-condemned" (Titus 3:10-11).

In her collection of poems entitled "Saints Without Tears," Phyllis McGinley has a poem called "The Temptation of St. Anthony":

"Off in the wilderness bare and level,
Anthony wrestled with the Devil.
Once he'd beaten the Devil down,
Anthony'd turn his eyes toward town
And leave his hermitage now and then
To come to grips with the souls of men.

Afterwards, all the tales agree,
Wrestling with the Devil seemed to be
Quite a relief to St. Anthony"*

Often it seems easier to "wrestle with the Devil" than it is

---

*From "The Love Letters of Phyllis McGinley." Used by permission of Viking Press.

to cope with difficult people who make life hard for us.

An American visiting the Moscow zoo was amazed to see a lion and a lamb in the same cage. "Do they get along well?" he asked the Russian guide. "They get along fine," replied the Russian, adding, "Of course, we have to put in a new lamb every day." There are lions and lambs among people, too. This prompted St. Paul to say in today's epistle lesson, "As for a man who is factious (troublesome), after admonishing him once or twice, have nothing more to do with him, knowing that such a person is . . . self-condemned" (Titus 3:10-11).

An eight-year-old wrote the following essay on Quakers: "Quakers are very meek, quiet people who never fight or answer back. My father is a Quaker, but my mother is not."

How Wars Begin

A boy once asked, "Dad, how do wars begin?" "Well, take the first World War," said his father. "That got started when Germany invaded Belgium." Immediately his wife interrupted him. "Tell the boy the truth. It began because somebody was murdered." The husband drew himself up with an air of superiority and snapped back, "Are you answering the question, or am I?" Turning her back upon him in a huff, his wife walked out of the room and slammed the door as hard as she could. When the dishes stopped rattling in the cupboard, an uneasy silence followed, broken at length by the son. "Daddy, you don't have to tell me how wars begin; I know now."

A person was surprised to find a pastor who had given up the ministry and was practicing medicine. When asked why he did this, the former pastor replied, "I took up the practice of medicine because I discovered that people will pay more money to care for their bodies than for their souls."

Some years later this same man gave up medicine and became an attorney. Explaining why, he said, "I took up the practice of law because I discovered that people will pay more money to get their own way than for either body or soul."

People insist on getting their own way—no matter what the price.

What Do We Do?

How do we deal with people who insist on their own way; people who are hard to get along with? What do we do after we have tried to be kind and loving, understanding and forgiving? What do we do after we have gone the second mile? What do we do when despite all our efforts at reconciliation they persist in their stubborness and hostility? St. Paul's answer is that after we have "admonished" such a person once or twice, i.e., really tried to communicate with him, and he persists in his stubborness, we are to "have nothing more to do with him." Let him know that you are maintaining an attitude of openness and love toward him, but if the other person insists on being a porcupine pricking anyone who comes close to him, let a respectable distance separate you.

St. Paul explains himself further when he writes in Romans 12:18, "If possible, so far as it depends on you, live peaceably with all." As far as you are concerned, live peaceably with all, if possible. But it does not always depend on you and because of this, it is not always possible. So "have nothing more to do with him."

An example of this is Elizabeth Barrett Browning who was disowned by her father when she married Robert. She sought to restore the relationship by writing a letter every week. After ten years of this one-way correspondence, she finally received a package from her father. To her dismay and heartbreak the parcel contained every letter she had written him. Not a single one had been opened. "If possible, so far as it depends on you, live peaceably with all."

You Are the Man!

One thing every Christian must consider is that this "factious," troublesome person that Paul speaks about in today's epistle lesson is not always someone else. Most often we are that person. It's like the person who has "halitosis." Everyone knows it except the person who has it. The trouble is that we can't see ourselves. We're constantly looking at other people's faults—never our own. We need to be like the disciples when Jesus announced to them that one of them would betray Him. Instead of pointing the finger at others, they asked, "Lord, is it I?"

So today we need to take a good look at ourselves. Am I the "factious" one in my home or at work? Perhaps people have been trying to "admonish" me? Perhaps a good deal of what I call their "nagging" or "bad temper" are just their attempts to make me see the truth. Of all the troublesome, "factious" people in my home or at my job, there is only one whom I can do anything about; only one whom I can change: me. So, let me concentrate on me. Let me bring "me" to Christ in humble repentance for my sins beseeching His power to make me a new person.

The Carpenter's Tools

I should like to close with a fable about a conversation that took place in a carpenter's shop.

Brother Hammer was in the chair. The meeting had informed him that he must leave because he was much too noisy. But he said, "If I am to leave this carpenter's shop, Brother Pencil must also go. He is so insignificant that he makes very little impression."

Little Brother Pencil arose and said, "All right, but Brother Screw must also go. You have to turn him around and around, again and again, to ever get him anywhere."

And Brother Screw said, "If you wish, I will go, but Brother Plane must leave also. All his work is on the surface. There is no depth to him."

And to this, Brother Plane replied, "Well, Brother Ruler

will have to go if I go, for he is always measuring other people as if he is the only one who is ever right."

Brother Ruler then complained against Brother Sandpaper and said, "I just don't care. He has to go, too. He is too rough and he's always rubbing people the wrong way."

And in the midst of this discussion the Carpenter of Nazareth walked in. He had come to perform his days' work. He put on his apron and went to his bench to make a table. He used the screw, the pencil, the sandpaper, the saw, the hammer, the plane, and all the other tools.

And after the day's work was over and the table finished, Brother Saw arose and said, "Brethren, I perceive that all of us are laborers together."

There was no accusation against one of these tools that was not absolutely true. And yet the Carpenter used every one of them. And there was not a place where he used any one of them where another one could have been used.

PRAYER

Lord, when I hear Paul speaking of troublesome people, I cannot but ask, "Lord, is it I?" I know that we are all imperfect tools in your hands, Lord, but we pray that You smooth the rough edges and make us more useable for the work of Your kingdom. Amen.

Can Human Nature Be Changed?

Fifth Sunday of Luke (Galatians 6:11-18)

"For neither circumcision counts for anything nor uncircumcision, but a new creation" (Gal. 6:15).

At an international meeting of psychologists, the question was raised: "Can we change human nature?"

One famous psychologist got up and said, "We have to raise the question, can we really modify or change human behavior? I look around this room and see that we are psychologists, yet we all probably eat too much, drink too much, smoke too much and move around too little. We know it, but we can't even change ourselves! How, then, can we hope to change others?"

An irate subscriber stormed into a newspaper office one day waving the current edition. He asked to see the man who wrote the obituary column. He was referred to a cub reporter to whom he showed the obituary column which included his name. "You can see I am very much alive. I demand a retraction!" Replied the reporter, "I never retract a story. But I'll tell you what I'll do; I'll put you in the birth column and give you a fresh start!"

It is about this "fresh start" that St. Paul speaks in today's epistle lesson: "For neither circumcision counts for anything nor uncircumcision, but a new creation" (Gal. 6:15).

"If only I could begin all over again. If only I could have a fresh start." This has been our plea since Adam. Jesus is God come to earth in answer to this plea. He came to give each one of us a fresh start.

Let a man go to a psychiatrist, but what can he become? An adjusted sinner. Let a man go to a physician, and what can he become? A healthy sinner. Let a man achieve wealth, and what can he become? A wealthy sinner. But let him go in sincere repentance and faith to the foot of the cross, and what can he become? A new creature in Christ Jesus, forgiven, reconciled, with meaning and purpose in his life and on the way to marvelous fulfillment in God's will.

The New Man

God's eternal Son became Man, and as a result, something happened to change the whole world. Jesus is not just a new man, a new specimen of the species. He is *the new Man*—God's own man to produce a whole crop of new men—men with a new mind and a new heart ready to go God's way at whatever cost to themselves.

As C. S. Lewis has put it in his book, "Beyond Personality," "Mere improvement is no redemption, though redemption always improves even here and now, and will, in the end, improve them to a degree we cannot yet imagine. God became Man to turn creatures into sons; not simply to produce better men of the old kind but to produce a new kind of man."*

A New Kind of People

Listen to this description of the early Christians as a new kind of people, written by the Athenian orator, Aristides, to the Roman Emperor Hadrian (117-138 A.D.):

"The Christians know and trust God. . . . They placate

---

*"Beyond Personality" by C. S. Lewis. Macmillan Co. Used by permission.

those who oppress them and make them their friends, they do good to their enemies. Their wives are absolutely pure, and their daughters modest. Their men abstain from unlawful marriage and are free from all impurity. If any of them have bondwomen or children, they persuade them to become Christians for the love they have toward them; and when they become so, they call them without distinction brothers. . . . They love one another. They do not refuse to help the widows. They rescue the orphan from him who does him violence. He who has, gives ungrudgingly to him who has not. If they see a stranger, they take him to their dwellings and rejoice over him as over a real brother; for they do not call themselves brothers after the flesh, but after the Spirit and in God. . . . If any one among them is poor and needy, and they do not have food to spare, they fast for two or three days, that they may supply him with necessary food. They scrupulously obey the commands of their Messiah. Every morning and every hour they thank and praise God for His loving-kindness toward them. . . . Because of them there flows forth all the beauty that there is in the world. But the good deeds they do, they do not proclaim in the ears of the multitude, but they take care that no one shall perceive them. Thus they labor to become righteous. . . . Truly, *this is a new people* and *there is something* divine in them." "A *new people* . . . something *divine in them.*" A new creation!

". . . Such Were Some of You"

Speaking of these "new people" St. Paul says, "Do not be deceived; neither the immoral, nor idolators, nor adulterers, nor homosexuals, nor thieves, nor the greedy, nor drunkards, nor revilers, nor robbers will inherit the kingdom of God. *And such were some of you. But you were washed, you were sanctified, you were justified* in the name of the Lord Jesus Christ and in the Spirit of our God" (I Cor. 6:9-11). They became "new creations" in Christ.

Can human nature be changed? Yes, in Christ.

One of the differences between the Old Testament and the New is this: the Old Testament says, "There is nothing new under the sun." In the New Testament Jesus says, "Behold, I make all things new."

A prison warden was told once, "Leopards don't change their spots." The warden, a deeply devoted Christian, who believed in the power of Christ to change people, replied, "Sir, I don't have any leopards in my prison. I only have people. And people change."

How?

But the question is *how* do people change?

How does one become a new creation? Paul gives us the answer when he says, "If any man is *in Christ*, he is a new creation." It begins with a *new birth* in Christ. "Truly, truly, I say to you," said Jesus, "unless one is born anew, he cannot see the kingdom of God" (John 3:3). This new birth was given to us in baptism. The line of our heredity was transferred from the old Adam line to the new Christ line. Life found a new origin, a new beginning, a new heredity in this new birth. We received the Holy Spirit. Our bodies became temples of God. The blood of Jesus now flows in our very veins through Holy Communion. We have become a new people: God's people.

But this new birth in Christ, because it happened when we were children, must be followed by a personal acceptance of Christ as our Lord and Savior.

Upon his conversion to Christ, Charles Colson wrote a book, "Born Again," in which he says,

"I was one of those individuals who went to church, studied in Sunday School, really I believed that I was a Christian. If someone asked what I was, I'd say, 'Sure, I'm a Christian. I'm not Jewish. What else can I be?' I'd learned about Christ but I hadn't learned what it really meant to take literally and seriously His claim upon my life. And what it means is to lay down my life and to really surrender my own will and stubborn pride, which was my problem for 40 years. And to simply say, Lord Jesus I accept You; I hear Your words; I want You to be my Savior; and even more important, I want You to be Lord of my life. And die to yourself, die daily as Paul wrote. And then you begin to feel the power that God will work through your life. It's the power of the Holy Spirit working through us, it isn't us."

After the new birth—baptism—must come this personal acceptance of Jesus as Lord and a personal commitment to Him as God. This is followed by repentance for our sins and a complete forsaking of the old life, after which our life is placed under new management. There is no better manager in this universe than the Lord Jesus Christ. The wisest and the best thing I can do with the life He gave me is to place it under His management. Then it will become truly new and a blessing to humanity.

A man when he is born is only a man. But a man when he is reborn in Christ is more. He is a new man with a new life and a new name. He is even named after Christ: CHRIST-ian!

"If any man is in Christ, he is a new creation—the old is passed and gone, and everything becomes fresh and new"—in Christ, under His management!

Not Always Instant

"We may be damned alone," said Alexei Khomiakov, "but we are saved together." We are saved in that *koinonia* which is the Church of Christ. We Orthodox believe that to be saved it is necessary for every human creature to find fellowship in the Church of Jesus Christ. She is "the Body of Christ." She is "the Vine," "the Sheepfold," "the Temple of the Holy Spirit." The Orthodox Church is the Ark of Salvation. She is the life of Christ extended to mankind. The New Life, initiated by Baptism and sustained by the Eucharist, becomes the way to follow as one walks through this world. This means that salvation, as a rule, is not always instant. It begins on the day of our baptism when we renounce the Devil, receive Christ, and accept the gift of the Holy Spirit. From that moment we begin a process of spiritual growth. The Sacraments of the Church provide us with the grace we need to become like God, deified, "partakers of divine nature" as St. Peter says.

We Are Called To Be Partakers of Divine Nature

The Eastern Church's doctrine of salvation teaches that Christ the Savior came to save not only *from* but also *for*. He came to save us *from* sin *for* participation in the life of God. This exalted vision of the Christian life was expressed by St. Peter when he wrote that we are invited "to become partakers of the Divine Nature" (2 Peter 1:4). It was also affirmed by St. Basil the Great when he described man as "the creature who has received an order to become god." The whole emphasis of the Orthodox way of life is on "putting on Christ" and receiving the Holy Spirit through prayer and the Sacraments so that we may begin to live a new life in union with Christ and in communion with the Holy Spirit.

Therefore, to be "born again" is a continuous condition of each person in the church. Perfection comes by acquisition of the Holy Spirit or, as St. Paul wrote, "by the washing, regeneration, and renewal of the Holy Spirit" (Titus 3:5). Thus, we do not become simply "good," "ethical" people but achieve gradually a new religious consciousness, a new level of being, becoming "a new creation in Christ Jesus." The Church creates the new man in the Sacraments and in the Truth Who is Christ.

Here is the only reconciling, healing force in the world today. We have tried every single one of the counterfeit humanist ideas that have hit the world broadside. For the last 100 years we've had every kind of philosophical answer to the problems of mankind. Not a single one of them works. Every single one of them is bankrupt. Only the healing power of

Jesus works. Only He could change a Saul into a Paul. It's the one healing power that can not only save planet earth from destroying itself but make it into "a new heaven and a new earth."

Try God

when troubles are deep
and your world is dark,
don't give up hope,
"TRY GOD" . . .

when life turns sour
and you've lost your way,
don't give up hope,
"TRY GOD" . . .

when fears stack up
and you're sure no one cares,
don't give up hope,
"TRY GOD" . . .

when temptation comes knocking
and you struggle with it so,
don't give up hope,
"TRY GOD" . . .

He can change you. He can make you new.

Whence Our Sense of Values?

Sixth Sunday of Luke (Galatians 1:11-19)

"For I would have you know, brethren, that the gospel which was preached is not man's gospel. For I did not receive it from man, nor was I taught it, but it came through a revelation of Jesus Christ" (Galatians 1:11-12).

A leading magazine editorialized recently: "At the heart of all this confusion lies the value vacuum. This is the great yawning void . . . . which (has) cast aside all principles and standards, leaving only chaos and dark night to rule over ruin. This is the absence of any belief in a universal and objective moral order. This is the total lack of any moral authority anywhere."

A psychiatrist tells of working with young people whom he found to be angry at their parents for not having given them a value system. He says, "I'm tired of wealthy people who give their children cars, but no moral values . . . saying they don't know what's wrong with their youngsters. What's wrong is that the parents are leading hollow, empty lives, and not giving their children anything to hold onto." Parents have failed to transmit to the young the standards of conduct which past generations had learned were necessary for a livable world.

The result is that everywhere today young people are

searching for new values, and a new life style. In their search they turn from drugs to Eastern religions to yoga to devil worship to the occult to astrology. Even popular music and art today express the idea that the external society is superficial and phony, that there is a deeper reality somewhere.

Shallowness Revealed

There are times when the shallowness of our values catches up with us. Shortly before he died, singer Nat King Cole said, "When you know you are dying, so-called big things become small things and the so-called small things become really the most important things." Another person facing death said, "My whole life changed. The things I valued most were now worthless, and the things I thought of little value, now became the most important things in the world to me." When the "Titanic" went down, a wealthy woman who had been flashing her diamonds around during the trip, took with her into the lifeboat, not her diamonds, but a bag of oranges. How values change in the face of death.

Source of Values

Centuries ago Aristotle said that the aim of education is to make pupils like or dislike what they should. There are some things we ought to like, and these constitute the values that remain forever valid.

The question arises: What is the source of these values? Let us consider the many answers to this question.

First, there are those who believe that there are no values at all. These are the people who in the words of Oscar Wilde know the price of everything and the value of nothing. The trouble with these people who believe that there are no values, however, is that they are constantly comparing things. They believe in good, better, best. How can we know that one thing is better than another unless we have some idea of the Best. If there are no absolute values, where does the idea of "Best" come from?

C. S. Lewis, the great Oxford atheist who found his way back to Christ, said, "My argument against God was that the universe seemed so cruel and unjust. But how had I got this idea of just and unjust? A man does not call a line crooked unless he has some idea of a straight line. What was I comparing this universe with when I called it unjust?"* He realized that the very idea of value of justice had to come from God Whom he was trying to deny.

Moreover, unless we are psychopaths we all believe in decent behavior. We believe in it so much that we make excuses when we fail to act decently. We blame it on others or on our mood. If there are no absolute values, where does this feeling that I *ought* to do certain things come from? Why is there this almost universal moral sense? Why do we consider that "good" is always better than "evil"?

There is a sense of moral values in us. It is part of the image of God in us.

Dr. Johnson said once about a certain philosopher, "If he really does think that there is no difference between right and wrong, why, Sir, when he leaves our house, let us count the spoons."

Individualism

It seems, then, that we are forced to believe in the existence of a real right and wrong. Even so, people differ as to the source of right and wrong. Some say that everyone has a right to decide his own values. Each person decides for himself in each situation what is right and what is wrong. If this be true; if everyone reserves the right to decide one's own standards, then we have absolutely nothing to say to a Hitler or a Stalin. For they did exactly the same. They determined for themselves what was right and wrong. They recognized no authority higher than themselves. Now this "authority" of the

---

"Mere Christianity" by C. S. Lewis. Paperback. Used by permission. The MacMillan Co.

self is no authority at all. We are at the mercy of what Sartre called "manufactured values" peculiar to the individual, altered and repudiated at the individual's whim; values according to which it is right to exterminate anyone—even millions of people if they stand in your way.

Dostoevsky said once that if man removes God from the throne of his life then he becomes god. He manufactures his own commandments and value system.

Relativism and Secularism

In addition to individualism another value system is called relativism. It is the conviction that there is no such thing as truth, or right and wrong, but only the varying beliefs of varying cultures, each justifying its own way of life.

Another value system is secularism—the belief that there is no reality higher or more lasting than the physical universe. No value is accepted as valid unless it can be certified and measured by the methods of science.

This, of course, leaves God out of the picture completely, since He is not small enough to be placed in a test tube and "verified" by science. The "manufactured values" of individualism, relativism, and secularism, all leave God out.

The "Gallup Poll" Value System

A final way of establishing a value system is the "Gallup Poll" method. If you want to know what is right and what is wrong, look at the average behavior of people in any culture. If most people are doing it, it's right. This is the method Kinsey used in his study of sex norms. According to this system, there may eventually be huge computers which will record what most people think and do at any one given moment, and this will become the law of the world.

Not Man's Gospel

St. Paul tells us in today's epistle lesson that the gospel he received is not man's gospel. It did not come from man. It did not originate in any individual. It is not the result of any Gallup Poll. It was not born from the spirit of any "golden" age. It was not kicked out of a computer. It came through a revelation of Jesus Christ (Gal. 1:12).

Speaking at M.I.T. some years ago, Winston Churchill said that Christians have the blessings of a *revealed religion.* Christianity is first and foremost a *revelation.* By revelation we mean that Christianity did not originate with man. It came from God. It was revealed to man from above. Our morals, our value system, our commandments, our guidelines, the principles we live by as Christians, come from God, not from man. They are revealed. They came through a revelation of Jesus Christ. The Apostle Peter says, ". . . no prophecy ever came by the impulse of man, but *man moved by the Holy Spirit spoke from God*" (2 Peter 1:21). And the Apostle Paul emphasized in today's epistle lesson: "For I would have you know, brethren, that the gospel which was presented by me is not man's gospel. For I did not receive it from man, nor was I taught it, *but it came through a revelation of Jesus Christ*" (Gal. 1:11-12).

When God chose to give man the ten commandments, He did not ask them to conduct a Gallup Poll among themselves to derive the *ought* from the *is*. Instead Moses climbed Mt. Sinai and there the ten commandments were given him by God engraved on stone tablets to signify that they were never to be changed. The commandments did not come up from earth, from man; they came down from above, from God, by divine revelation.

"I am from above," said Jesus. From above He brings us God's answers to the most vexing questions of life: Who am I? Where am I going? Why am I here? What's my purpose in life?

"I am from above." From above Christ brings us God's light for our darkness, God's forgiveness for our sins, God's truth for our confusion, God's comfort for our sorrow, God's strength for our weakness.

God Has Not Left Us Alone

We live in a sea of right and wrong, but God has not left us without chart or compass. Praised be His Name! The flight to the moon could not have been accomplished without "mission control" in Houston. The space men were in constant communication with their home base. If they had lost contact, they would have vanished—perhaps forever. One scientist said, "When Apollo II malfunctioned, without the computer it would have taken 90,000 years to find a new flight plan."

If control and guidance are important on a flight to the moon, how much more important for our journey through this life to eternity. Yet the good news is that God has not left us alone in this journey. He has given us guidance. He gave us Jesus to be our "mission control." In constant contact with Him, guided and filled with the Holy Spirit, we know the way; we know what the real values of life are.

A scientist said once that what led him to Christ was that science had nothing to say about values, about what is best in life, about what we ought to choose. This he found in Christ.

If the Christian is out of step with the confused values of this world, it is because he marches to the music of a different drummer: the Lord Jesus. He is the One Who reveals to us values that never change, the eternal values of God. As He Himself said, "I am the Way, the Truth, and the Life; no man comes to the Father except through me."

The Perfect Diamond

A diamond assessor has a difficult job. Surrounded by dozens of trays of finished diamonds, he has to determine their value and place them in a tray marked with a certain price.

One day an assessor was asked, "How is it you can look all day at hundreds of diamonds without becoming confused? How do you maintain your sense of values?"

The assessor smiled, "It's very simple, friend," he replied.

Holding out his hand, he pointed to a fabulous diamond ring on his finger. "This diamond is perfect," he said. "It doesn't have a single flaw. Every half hour or so, I put it under my eyeglasses. The picture of the perfect diamond restores my sense of values!"

What the flawless diamond was to the assessor, the Lord Jesus is to us. By looking constantly at Him and measuring all things in the light of His perfection and His commandments, we keep a sense of what is really important and what is not, what is right and what is wrong, what is eternal and what is temporal, what is expensive and what is cheap, what deserves our allegiance and what does not.

Not a Human Revelation

Our way of life as Christians is not based on the opinions of great thinkers or philosophers. It is not based on relativism or secularism or individualism or the Gallup Poll. Our way of life is based *on God's divinely revealed will for us*. For God has spoken in Christ. He was the One Who spoke to Paul. He is the One Who speaks to us today. As the voice of God said at the transfiguration on Mt. Tabor, "He (Jesus) is my beloved Son, *listen to Him*!"

PRAYER

Heavenly Father, above the confusing, distracting voices the life. He alone speaks to us today by divine revelation to bring us Your plan for our lives. Amen.

BUT GOD . . .

Seventh Sunday of Luke (Ephesians 2:4-10)

"But God, Who is rich in mercy, out of the great love with which He loved us, even when we were dead through our trespasses, made us alive together with Christ . . ." Ephesians 2:4

Having built his bigger barns the rich farmer thought he would say to himself, "Soul, you have ample goods laid up for many years; take your ease, eat, drink, and be merry." Bigger barns—he thought—would bring him to the pinnacle of success. Then all of a sudden comes that all-important conjunction "*BUT*." And what a difference it makes. "*BUT GOD* said to him, 'Fool! This night your soul is required of you; and the things you have prepared, whose will they be?' " (Luke 12:20)

That farmer was no fool in things material; but he was a fool in things eternal. He never considered God, nor his soul, nor his fellow man, nor eternity. He thought he was sitting on top of the world. He thought he was successful. "*BUT GOD* said . . . Fool!"

The Difference

"But" is a conjunction with a difference!

A bee can never be an eagle, *but* it can make honey.

"And" is also a conjunction, *but* it doesn't carry the same impact as "but." To say "and" is to give additional information, but it is not information that changes the meaning of the preceding statement. "But" is different. Not only does it add more information, but it also changes the meaning of what has already been said.

For example, we say: "That is a good idea, *but* . . ." "He is a good businessman, *but* . . ." "She is a good friend, *but* . . ." The "but" keeps butting in to change the whole situation.

When the late Charles Evans Hughes, in his capacity as Secretary of State, attended a Pan-American Conference, he instructed his interpreter to give him a summarized translation of what was being spoken in Spanish or Portuguese, but he said, "While a running translation is ample for my purpose, I want you to give me a literal translation of every word after the speaker says *but*." What follows "but" is of the utmost importance!

This is true in our reading of the Bible. Again and again we come upon the expression "But God . . ." Whatever may have been said before is immediately qualified and often corrected by that which follows the conjunction "but."

"But God Who Is Rich in Mercy . . ."

For example, in today's Epistle lesson we read, "Among these we all once lived in the passions of our flesh, following the desires of body and mind, and so we were by nature children of wrath, like the rest of mankind." Then we come to these two words again, "But God," and how they change completely the meaning of the verse we just read. We may have been sinners living according to the passions of the flesh, says Paul, "*BUT GOD*, who is rich in mercy, out of the great love with which he loved us, even when we were dead through our trespasses, made us alive together with Christ . . . and raised us up with him, and made us sit with him in the heavenly places in Christ Jesus, that in the coming ages he might show the immeasurable riches of his grace in kindness toward us in Christ Jesus" (Eph. 2:3-7).

We had no way to escape the bondage of the devil or to rise out of spiritual death into the life of God; *but God* had.

Helpless But . . .

We were helpless sinners, says Paul in Romans 5:6. Then come those two words again, "*But God* shows his love for us in that while we were yet sinners Christ died for us."

"But now, having been freed from sin, you have become servants of God."

"But now in Christ Jesus, you who were once far off have been brought near in the blood of Christ."

"For the wages of sin is death." Then comes the great "but" of God's love: "but the free gift of God is eternal life in Jesus Christ our Lord" (Romans 6:23).

No matter how sinful we are, how unworthy or inferior we consider ourselves, God's forgiving love can hardly wait to bestow upon the penitent sinner the immeasurable riches of His grace.

Sin? Yes! But God's mercy is greater than any sin.

The Great "But" in Joseph's Life

We read in Genesis 39:20-21,

"And Joseph's master took him and put him into the prison, the place where the king's prisoners were confined, and he was there in prison.*But the Lord* was with Joseph, and showed him steadfast love, and gave him favor in the sight of the keeper of the prison."

It seems that everyone and everything was against Joseph. His older brothers hated him and wanted to take his life; they sold him into a living death as a slave in Egypt. Falsely accused, he was cast into prison. He was an alien, a slave in a strange land, a prisoner, without a friend in the world. Then comes that great "but" of God's love: "*But* the Lord was with Joseph." The Lord saw to it that the evil committed against him worked out to his good. As Joseph himself told his brothers later, "As for you, you meant evil against me, *but God* meant it for good . . . "

The whole world was against Joseph, *but God* was with him.

Life does terrible things to us. We suffer broken hopes, moral failures, profound denials. *But God* is able to bring good even out of evil to those who love Him and cooperate with Him.

The Psalmist

"My flesh and my heart may fail," says the Psalmist (73:26) "*but God* is the strength of my heart and my portion forever."

The entire psalm hinges on the single word *but*. Up to that point there seemed to be no real help for God's troubled servant; *but God* proved Himself to be the strength of his heart and his portion forever. Then tears turned to triumph, bewilderment to blessings, and perplexity to praise.

"O Lord, how many are my foes!
Many are rising against me;
many are saying of me,
there is no help for him in God."
Then come those two words again:
"But thou, O Lord, art a shield
about me,
My glory, and the lifter of my head" (Psalm 3:1-3).

"I was pushed hard, so that I was falling,
but the Lord helped me.
The Lord is my strength and my song;
He has become my salvation" (Psalm 118:14).

Weak? Yes! Helpless? No! *But God* is my strength and my salvation!

Peter

Jesus said to Simon Peter one day,

"Simon, Simon, behold, Satan demanded to have you, that he might sift you like wheat, *but I* have prayed for you that your faith may not fail; and when you have turned again, (to) strengthen your brethren" (Luke 22:31-32). In time of deepest darkness and despair Jesus wanted Peter to know that He cared. He prayed for him to be restored and to become a channel of strength for his fellow believers.

Temptation? Yes! We live with it every day, *but God* prays for us to overcome! We are tested, but not forsaken; bruised, but not abandoned; utterly cast down, but not destroyed, because of Him who says to us today as He did to Peter long ago: "But I have prayed for you that your faith may not fail."

When we come to the end of our Lord's life, we read,

"And when they had fulfilled all that was written of him, they took him down from the cross and laid him in a tomb."

That was to be the end of the greatest life ever lived. That was to be the period at the end of life—death!

But wait! Here comes another one of those great "buts" of God—only this time it is the greatest "but" every spoken:

"*But God* raised him from the dead" (Acts 13:20-30).

PRAYER

The world may press in upon me, Lord, but You make the difference. I am weak *but* in You I find strength. I am tempted *but* in You I find a way out. I despair *but* in You I find hope. Help me to cling to You. Amen.

Who's Perfect?

Eighth Sunday of Luke (Hebrews 7:26-8:2)

Who's perfect?

In a conversation with some friends last week, a person was criticized for some failure. The person who was criticized quickly replied, "Well, I can't be perfect at everything."

Cardinal Newman said once, "Nothing would be done at all if a man waited till he could do it so well that no one would find fault with him." "He who makes no mistakes never makes anything," says a proverb.

No one should expect perfection from oneself or from others. Bruce Barton said once, "If you expect perfection from people, your whole life is a series of disappointments, grumblings and complaints. If, on the contrary, you pitch your expectations low, taking folks as the inefficient creatures which they are, you are frequently surprised by having them perform better than you had hoped."

Mickey Mantle earned $100,000 a year because he made three of every ten hits. He missed seven out of every ten hits.

Who's perfect?

No one. But we expect perfection from others, like the person who walked into a restaurant and said to the waitress: "Two eggs please. Don't fry them a second after the white is cooked. Don't turn them over. Not too much grease. Just a pinch of salt. No pepper. Well, waitress, what are you waiting for?" The waitress stared at him and said, "The hen's name is Eleanor—is that all right?"

Excellence Versus Perfection

Dr. DeBakey, the famous heart surgeon, said, "I plead guilty to being a perfectionist. That patient on the table is a living human being. His heart, his life is in our hands, and a single mistake can kill him. I have to be a perfectionist."

One cannot but admire such a surgeon. Yet the truth is that there is a difference between striving for excellence and striving for perfection. The first—striving for excellence—is attainable, gratifying, and healthy. The second—striving for perfection—is often unattainable, frustrating and neurotic. It is unrealistic to expect anyone to be perfect all the time.

The stenographer who retypes a lengthy letter because of a trivial error, or the boss who demands such retyping, might profit from examining the Declaration of Independence. When the writer of that document made two errors of omission, he inserted the missing letters between the lines. If this is acceptable in the document that gave birth to American freedom, surely, it should be acceptable in a letter that will be briefly glanced at en route to someone's wastebasket.

Socrates was wryly realistic when he said, "I have discovered Utopia, but I can find no perfect man to bring into it."

It's true that nature didn't make us perfect, but she did the next best thing, she made us blind to our faults. Thus, some of us go through life thinking we're perfect.

Yet, as the Country Parson said, "A fellow shouldn't hide his faults too carefully. Perfection in others is not easy to admire." People don't admire perfection in others. They think it's unreal. Even the best speaker should make a mistake once in a while to show that he's human like the rest of us.

To Much Insistence on Perfection

A sixteen-year-old girl took an overdose of medication to

kill herself because she could not stand herself. A wise counselor discovered that she was trying to live up to the expectations of a mother who was a perfectionist. The girl tried to earn her mother's approval, and never got it.

Too much insistence on perfection can be destructive. Every child should grow up feeling it's not a tragedy to make a mistake.

No Perfect Marriages

Many couples enter marriage with expectations that are altogether too idealistic. Imperfect people marry imperfect people and then begin to expect perfection from one another. We expect from our spouse the kind of perfection that belongs only to God. A husband said to his wife one day, "Young lady, you made a grave mistake. You married a man instead of an archangel." No marriages are made in heaven. They come in kits and we have to put them together. A perfect wife is one who doesn't expect a perfect husband. One wife said to her husband one day, "If you weren't such a perfectionist, you'd be a perfect husband." I guess we need to remember that love has eyelids as well as eyes.

No Perfect Christians

Just as there are no perfect families or marriages, so there are no perfect Christians.

A stranger came into town on a Sunday morning and looked around for a church to attend. While standing outside one church he heard the minister and the congregation reading together: "We have left undone the things we ought to have done, and we have done the things we ought not have done."

He hesitated no longer, went inside, and dropped into a seat, sighing: "Thank goodness, I've found my kind of people at last."

In all other religions one has to be perfect in order to come to God. In Christianity one does not. One comes admitting he is a sinner but not wanting to remain one. He comes to the Savior asking to be forgiven and cleansed. Christ did not die for us because we are perfect but because we aren't. The perfect person needs no Savior. We cling to God's grace. He loves us in spite of our sins. "The saints," someone said, "are the sinners who keep on trying." The Church has never been a museum for the exhibition of perfect Christians, but always a hospital for the healing of ailing and imperfect Christians.

The Lord did not commit Himself to loving only perfect people. Just the opposite! He said, "I come not to call the righteous (the perfect), but sinners to repentance." He served those who desperately needed to grow up in the knowledge of God. Not only did He not despise them but He said, "There is more joy in heaven over one sinner who repents than over ninety nine who do not."

Does Christianity Demand Perfection?

An unbeliever said once, "Religion demands of a man that he be morally perfect, which is impossible. When a man fails in his frail attempts to be perfect, his religion then reacts on his spirits as a destructive force filling him with guilt and regrets."

Too many of us, I'm afraid, share this unbeliever's view of Christianity which is totally false. It does not take perfectionism to please God. He accepts me sinful though I am and forgives me. The way to reach God is not by climbing the ladder of perfection. He has already come down the ladder to meet me. I meet Him not on the topmost rung of the ladder with a prideful, "I thank You, God, that I am not like those other men who are below me on the ladder. . . . " I meet Him on the bottom-most rung of the ladder with the humble plea, "God, be merciful to me a sinner."

Who's Perfect?

If there are no perfect people, no perfect Christians, is there any such thing as perfection? There most certainly is! This is what the Epistle lesson today is all about. "For it was fitting that we should have such a high priest, holy, blameless, unstained, separated from sinners, exalted above the heavens. He has no need, like those high priests, to offer sacrifices daily, first for His own sins and then for those of the people; He did this once for all when he offered up himself" (Hebrews 7:26-27). He was the only High Priest Who was "holy, blameless, unstained, separated from sinners, exalted above the heavens," Who had no need to offer sacrifices for His own sins, for He had none. He is the only Perfect One.

We are to leave perfection to Christ. He is God. According to the ancient Greeks to "know thyself" meant to know that you are human; you are not God.

"You Must Be Perfect . . . "

Yes, but did not Jesus say, "You must be perfect even as your Father in heaven is perfect"? Does He not thus expect us to be perfect? It is regrettable that the words of Jesus "You *shall be* perfect" were translated as "You *must be* perfect." The Greek verb "eseste" used in the original Greek is a verb in the future tense. It is a promise which says very clearly that perfection is to be granted in the future by grace. In the English translation it is incorrectly translated in the present tense and in the imperative mood implying that man is expected to reach perfection now. It is not you *must* be perfect but you *shall be* perfect.

Perfection in this life according to Orthodox theology is not the state of "I have arrived. I have made it. I am saved." Rather, it is the state of "I am on the way. I am moving. I am growing." Man's life is never complete even in the Kingdom of God. We shall always be "on the way." Our very perfection is always to grow more perfect, more like unto Christ. And this is a never-ending process.

Movement Toward Perfection

To be as perfect as God is impossible for us. But to keep moving toward this perfection is always within our possibility with the help of God. In Orthodox spirituality, salvation is not a state of being; it is the motion toward theosis, toward becoming like God, which can never be fully achieved. It is growth in perfection. It is moving from sin to Christ, from slavery to freedom, from darkness to light, from falsehood to truth, from despair to hope, from death to life. And once we have reached truth, it is moving from truth to greater truth, from wisdom to greater wisdom, from joy to deeper joy, from understanding to deeper understanding, from all-embracing love to more all-embracing love. And this process goes on eternally. We can never reach the point where we can say, "Well, now I've made it. I just have to sit around and be perfect."

From the Lives of Saints

There was a very holy monk on Mt. Athos. All the monks revered him and tried to imitate his holiness. When asked about his holiness, the revered monk replied, "I've only just begun, my son. I've only just begun."

Abbott Sisois, who had spent 80 years in the desert, was dying at age 100. He lived a life of repentance. Tears of penitence had deeply scarred his radiant face. Yet at 100, he was asking God for more time to repent. His disciples were amazed. "You are asking for time to repent, you who are the master of repentance." The old saint replied, "I'm only just beginning to learn that art." After 80 years of unprecedented spiritual growth, he had still not reached perfection. He was still excited about growing, realizing his unlimited possibilities in Christ.

Reaching Higher Plateaus

About 400 years before Christ a gifted Greek named

Timanthes took instruction in art from a well-known tutor. After several years the budding young painter created an exquisite picture. When he was commended for his accomplishment, he became so enraptured with what he had produced that he sat day after day just gazing at the portrait. He mistakenly believed he would never be able to advance beyond that point. One morning when he went to admire his work again, he discovered that the master had blotted it out. Angry, and in tears, Timanthes ran to him and asked him why he had destroyed his cherished possession. The wise man replied, "I did it for your own good. That painting was retarding your progress. While it was an excellent piece of art, it was not perfect—even though it appeared that way to you. Start again and see if you can do even better!" The student took his advice and produced his greatest masterpiece called "Sacrifice of Iphigenia," which is regarded as one of the finest paintings of all antiquity.

Our Master in Heaven never wants us to be content with our accomplishments, no matter how able or perfect they may appear to us. He would have us reach even higher plateaus of service and holiness. St. Paul recognized this. That is why he said, "Not that I . . . am already perfect; *but I press on . . .* " (Phil. 3:12).

PRAYER

Dear Lord, keep me from thinking that I have arrived. Keep me moving, growing more and more like unto Thee. Amen.

What Is Grace?

Ninth Sunday of Luke (Ephesians 4:1-7)

"But grace was given to each of us according to the measure of Christ's gift" (Ephesians 4:7).

Karl Barth, the great theologian, was preaching to prisoners on New Year's Eve. He said, "Some of you have heard that over the last forty years I have written many books, many of them very fat ones. Yet there are four words which say it better than all the books I have written. These four words are 'my grace is enough.' When my books are forgotten, these words will shine in all their eternal richness."

"My grace is enough."

What is grace? It is perhaps one of the sweetest and most beautiful words in any language. The word "grace" suggests beauty, gladness, love, and kindness. There is more of Christianity poured into this one word than in any other.

The "grace of God" is one of the most beautiful expressions in our Christian vocabulary.

What is grace? What does it mean?

Definitions of God's Grace

Grace is God's loving activity in the world. It represents the unlimited pouring out of God's mercy. Grace is God's unconditional forgiveness offered to the unworthy. It is God's enabling power given to match and overcome the challenges of life.

Grace is God's love reaching out even to a thief dying on a cross, forgiving him in the last moment of his life, and saying to him, "Today, you will be with me in heaven."

"Grace is God's acceptance of that which is rejected," said Paul Tillich.

Grace does not say, "Go, and sin no more and I will not condemn you." It says, "Neither do I condemn you. Go and sin no more" (John 8:11).

Grace is that quality in God which moves Him to do good to us even though we do not deserve it. It is the opposite of justice.

Grace is God's giving of Himself to man. Grace is not a "thing" which God gives us. It is divine life itself; God coming to make His home in us. When God made us, He gave us ourselves. When He gives us grace, He gives us Himself.

Grace is not hesitating to go to God because I am not good enough. I dare to go not because I am good (I'm not), but because He is good and loves me despite my sins.

Grace is the invitation of Jesus: "Come to me all you who labor and are heavy laden and I will give you rest. Take my yoke upon you, and learn from me; for I am gentle and lowly in heart, and you will find rest for your souls" (Matt. 11:28-29).

Grace is the promise that in a world where there is crucifixion, the final word is resurrection. In a world where there is death, the final word is life.

Grace is the father of the prodigal son, standing in the doorway every night, straining his eyes, hoping he would see his son returning home. "But while he was yet at a distance, his father saw him and had compassion, and ran and embraced him and kissed him." That is grace!

Grace is God accepting me as His child in Baptism, filling me with His Holy Spirit in Confirmation, and then sending

Jesus to live in my heart through Holy Communion.

Dr. Paul Tournier wrote of grace:

"There comes a day when a man understands that all is of grace, that the whole world is a gift of God, a completely generous gift since no one forced Him to do it. We see each flower, each drop of water, each minute of our life as a gift of God . . . The great gift, the unique and living one, is not a thing but a person. It is Jesus Christ himself. In Him, God has given Himself, no longer just things which he creates or has created, but his own person, his own suffering, and his own solitude, given unto death itself."

Grace is Jesus on the cross saying to us, "You may grieve me; you may be disloyal to me; you may misunderstand me; you may batter me, bruise me, scourge me; you may treat me with savage injustice; you may even kill me on a cross, but I will never stop loving you. 'Father, forgive them, for they know not what they do.' "

Grace is another word for love except that it carries the additional meaning that the love is totally unmerited, completely unearned, and absolutely undeserved. It can be called "in-spite-of" love, because it is offered and given in spite of the fact that its recipient in no way deserves it.

Grace is what St. Paul experienced when he wrote, " . . . I formerly blasphemed and persecuted and insulted him; but I received mercy because I had acted ignorantly in unbelief, *and the grace of our Lord overflowed for me* with the faith and love that are in Christ Jesus" (I Tim. 1:13-14).

Grace is what Jesus did for us: "For you know the grace of our Lord Jesus Christ, that though he was rich, yet for your sake he became poor, so that by his poverty, you might become rich" (2 Cor. 8:9).

Grace is not accepting sin as the final word, but God's mercy. "Where sin abounded, grace did the more abound," says Paul.

Grace is not that we loved God. "In this is love, not that

we loved God but that he loved us and sent his Son to be the expiation for our sins" (I John 4:10). "We love because he first loved us" (I John 4:19). He took the initiative. He started it all by loving us first when we were unlovable. "But God shows his love for us in that while we were yet sinners Christ died for us" (Romans 5:8).

An elderly woman lay moaning and groaning on her death bed. She was afraid to die because she feared God would punish her for her many sins. The priest held a crucifix before her. "What does this mean to you?" he asked.

She replied, "That is the blessed Lord suffering on the cross—and, oh, dear, I will have to suffer too."

"Just a minute," said the priest. "You have it all wrong. This is Jesus dying on the cross, and He is suffering, but He is doing it all for you because He loves you. If you have to suffer, too, then all He did is wasted. He died to pay the penalty for your sins, so you won't have to be punished. All you have to do is confess your sins to Him and thank Him for His sacrificial love. After that, your past will be wiped out and you can look forward to a glorious future in eternity."

That is grace!

Not a Wage We Earn

Grace is a gift rather than a wage we earn. It cannot be deserved. Sin gives wages. God gives grace. "For the wages of sin is death, but the free gift of God is eternal life in Christ Jesus our Lord" (Romans 6:23). "For by grace you have been saved through faith; and this is not your own doing, it is the gift of God—not because of works, lest any man should boast" (Eph. 2:8). We cannot boast or look down on other human beings, because we are what we are as Christians only by the grace of God. Not by works but by grace through faith are we saved.

It is not we who work for God; it is God Who works through us. Who can ever boast? Who can ever put God in his debt? The typical parishioner, for example, feels that he has done something which puts God in his debt if he puts down a nice thick carpet in church or donates the biggest icon—a sort of afterlife insurance policy. But Jesus said, "So you also, when you have done all that is commanded you, say, 'We are unworthy servants; we have only done what was our duty' " (Luke 17:10).

Only By God's Grace

There is a story about a man who went to heaven. He was met at the pearly gates by Peter, who said, "It will take 1,000 points for you to be admitted. The good works you did during your lifetime will determine your points."

The man said, "Unless I was sick, I attended church every Sunday, and I sang in the choir."

"That will be 50 points," Peter said.

"And I gave to the church liberally," the man added.

"That is worth 25 more points," said Peter.

The man, realizing that he had only 75 points, started getting desperate. "I taught a Sunday school class," he said. "That's a great work for God."

"Yes," said Peter. "That's worth 25 points."

The man was frantic. "You know," he said, "at this rate the only way I'm going to get into heaven is by the grace of God."

Peter smiled. "That's 900 points! Come on in!"

In this world we get what we pay for, people say. Do we? What can we ever pay for the grace of God? What can we ever pay for His love? What can we ever pay for His sacrifice on the cross?

Accept It!

This great combination of love—the gift of His Son—and grace, which is that love in action, require a humble acceptance on our part. It was God's part to make grace available, which He has done. It is our part to accept it by thanking Him, praising Him, and resting our lives upon it.

Failure to accept the grace God provides is another form of sin. Francis of Assisi was asked one day, "What are you doing, Brother Francis?" "Sinning," he replied. "What! You who are our pattern and our leader, you sinning? How can that be?" Francis replied, "What else are we doing when we do not receive the grace of God as freely as it is offered?"

The Fruits of Grace

What a change takes place when I accept the fact that I am accepted. When I receive God's grace in faith, I become a new person in Christ. God's grace makes me a "gracious" person reaching out to others with the compassion, the unconditional concern, the free and undeserved acceptance that I myself have known in Christ.

The Austrian poet, Victor Daley, was cared for in a Roman Catholic hospital before his death. One of his last acts was to thank the nuns for all their kindnesses to him. "Don't thank us," said their leader. "Thank the grace of God." "But aren't you the grace of God?" the poet asked.

Grace has its fruits: it produces graciousness in us. When people irritate us—God's grace—enables us to respond with love and understanding. When problems arise—God's grace enables us to look beyond the problems to the One Who has the solution. When suffering comes—God's grace is more than enough to see us through the valley of the shadow to the shining Presence beyond.

One of the great fruits of grace is obedience; for, obedience is nothing but gratitude for grace. Perhaps the greatest blessing to flow from God's grace is "the peace of God which passes all understanding" (Phil. 4:7). This peace floods the hearts of those who rest in God's grace. The world cannot give such peace, nor take it away. It is the gift of God to those who have turned body, mind and soul over to Him.

Wrap Yourself Up In God's Grace

We need to wrap ourselves up in the grace of God every day just as the little child when it becomes afraid, wraps itself up in its mother's apron, has a good cry and is so comforted and strengthened that he jumps happily into the street again.

How do we know God's grace is true? We can take God's word for it because He has sealed His promise of grace with the blood of His Son.

Little wonder that the Bible concludes its revelation to man with the crowning act of all the ages: "The grace of our Lord Jesus Christ be with you all. Amen." (Rev. 22:21).

PRAYER

Dear Lord, You are the God of all grace:
justifying grace for the sinner,
illuminating grace for the confused,
comforting grace for the bereaved,
strengthening grace for the weak,
living grace for those who seek fulfillment,
dying grace for those who come to the end of life's journey.
Truly, Your grace is enough, sufficient for every need. Amen.

On Replacing Walls With Bridges

Tenth Sunday of Luke (Galatians 3:23 to 4:15).

"There is neither Jew nor Greek (the dividing wall of nation and race); there is neither slave nor free (the wall of class hatred); there is neither male nor female (the barrier of sex); for you are all one in Christ Jesus" (Gal. 3:28).

"Something there is that doesn't love a wall, that wants it down," said Robert Frost.

The world today takes issue with these familiar words of Robert Frost. There is something that loves a wall, something deep within the heart of man. Christ may have torn down the walls separating us from God and from each other, but we continue to build new barriers because of our sinfulness.

In the past, there was the Great Wall of China, 1500 miles of it, built to keep out the Mongolian horsemen, which it failed to do. Then there was Hadrian's Roman wall in England to stop the Picts and the Scots; eventually it was overrun.

Today we have walls in the Middle East, Cyprus, Vietnam, India and Pakistan. We have the "Iron Curtain", the "Bamboo Curtain", and perhaps the most famous (or infamous) of all—the Berlin Wall.

"Something there is that doesn't love a wall," said Robert Frost. But it seems that he was very wrong. There is something in man that must love walls; for there are walls everywhere separating and antagonizing the human race.

Not all the walls in the world are made of brick and mortar. There are other kinds of walls, invisible walls, walls of suspicion and hatred; walls in the minds and hearts of men; walls between the races; between the young and the old; the haves and the have-nots, the liberals and the conservatives, labor and management; walls that block communication and separate parent from child, husband from wife, Christian from Christian, nation from nation, man from God. It is no wonder that someone has described our time as "the pathetic age of partition."

Walls Between Parents and Children

There are the walls between parents and children.

A certain father is having trouble "reaching" his teenage son. He speaks to the boy only in a complaining mood. He criticizes the boy's hair style, clothing, and companions. He finds fault with most everything his son says or does.

It may be a long time before this father "reaches" the boy. For he is building a wall with the bricks of bickering and the concrete of contempt. By his constant nagging he is making that wall all the more solid and higher.

Like many other people, this father does not realize that the way to "reach" people is by building bridges rather than walls—bridges of careful listening and patient understanding.

Walls In Marriage

There are walls in marriage. There is one point we emphasize to all couples in pre-marital counseling. That is, never to let "the sun go down on your anger." If you've had a misunderstanding, never let the day come to a close without resolving that disagreement, without talking about it, and forgiving each other. Every unresolved conflict is like a brick. Over a period of months and years these bricks begin to accumulate. Soon they begin to take shape forming a Berlin Wall, running right through the middle of the home. The husband finds himself living on one side of the wall, and the wife on the other wide with no communication between them. One husband confessed, "There's a big wall between us, built by both of us. It's so high we can hardly see each other any more." This is one of the most tragic walls; a wall that brings great heartache and often leads to divorce.

Walls of Race

There are the walls of race. In this day and age, when we lament the Berlin Wall, we have walls running right through the middle of our cities; walls that separate us from our neighbors; walls of bias and bigotry. William James said once, "A great many people think they are thinking when they are merely rearranging their prejudices." Prejudices build walls.

How much we need to heed the words of Edwin Markham:

"He drew a circle that shut me out—
Heretic, rebel, a thing to flout.
But love and I had the wit to win;
We drew a circle that took him in."

"A new commandment I give to you," said Jesus, "that you love one another as I have loved you."

Walls Between Persons

There are walls between persons. People who have been hurt by others build walls to protect their ego. A woman who has been "hurt" by one man, takes a vow never to trust *any man again.* A child who has had his ego sliced up by a cruel parent or teacher, takes a vow never to trust *any authority* figure in the future. A man who has had his love rejected by *one woman* may take a vow never to become emotionally involved with *any human being* in the future. The emotional wall that we build as protection against *one person,* cuts us off from all other human beings. We literally wall ourselves in and then criticize our neighbors because they do not climb over the wall to come to us. The result is loneliness both in us and in others. People are lonely because they build walls instead of bridges.

The Wall of Unforgiveness

There is the great wall of unforgiveness. Jesus told the story of the servant who was forgiven a great debt, but who, in turn, refused to forgive a *small* debt to his fellow servant, and had him thrown in prison for non-payment. The unforgiving spirit erects walls between people, but it also sets up a barrier between a man and his God. For, as Jesus said, "If you do not forgive men their trespasses, neither will your Father forgive your trespasses" (Matthew 6:15).

If there are long-standing walls of hostility and hatred in our lives, separating us from loved ones and others, they can be destroyed if we will take the initiative to forgive as we have been forgiven by Christ. Forgiveness is the great destroyer of walls. It builds bridges.

A judge in a family court tells how every day he tries to help husbands and wives tear down their walls, their spite fences, and build bridges of mutual love and respect.

Archbishop Bloom tells of a man of some standing who once came to see him. He told him that a friend . . . had offended him: "Who should go and make his peace with the other?" he asked. "I cannot answer your question," replied the Archbishop, "as I cannot possibly set myself as a judge between you, but one thing is certain to me: the meanest of the two of you will wait for the other to make the move." The great man said no word, but went immediately to replace the wall of hostility with a bridge of love.

Aristippus and Aeschines were two ancient Greeks who were friends. Aristippus was a famous philosopher. Anger arose between them. Someone asked Aristippus: 'Where now is the friendship of you two?" "It is asleep," said Aristippus, "but I will awaken it." So he went to Aeschines. "Do I appear to you," he asked, "so utterly unfortunate and incurable as not to be able to receive correction from you?" And Aeschines moved by his friend's humility forgot his anger.

It takes humility to say: "Please tell me my faults." It takes humility to ask for criticism, but it is the way to learn about ourselves, to grow in grace. It is the way to forgiveness; the way to tear down walls and build bridges.

The Wall Between Man and God

The greatest of all walls in history, was the wall between God and man as symbolized by the temple veil in the Old Testament which separated the Holy of holies or the presence of God from the people. The Holy of holies was off limits to everyone except the high priest, and even he was allowed to enter only once a year. The moment Jesus died "the veil of the temple was rent in two from the top to the bottom" (Matthew 27:51). The wall of separation was demolished. God and man were reconciled. Through Jesus we now have complete access to God. Jesus is the One who opens for us the way to God. "For he is our peace, who has made us both one, and has broken down the dividing wall of hostility . . . So then you are no longer strangers . . . but you are fellow citizens with the saints and members of the household of God" (Eph. 2:14, 19).

Let me share a vivid picture of this reconciliation. A story is told of a young boy who lay dying in a hospital. His worst hurt was not that he was dying but that his father and mother were separated and fighting each other. One day they both came to see him at the same time. This created a most awkward situation. They stood on opposite sides of the bed. The dying boy took the hand of his mother on one side of the bed, and the hand of his father on the other side. Then he asked them to pray. What an embarassing moment! They could not pray. The little boy's eyes were tear-filled and pleading. The tense father had to do something. He did. He reached across the bed with his free hand toward the child's mother. She responded by reaching out her free hand from her side and took his hand. Now they were in an unbroken circle. Now they both could pray and cry out for forgiveness and mercy. Out of their little boy's death came reconciliation, love, healing and new life.

Jesus died to reconcile us to Himself. "But now in Christ Jesus you who once were far off have been brought near in the blood of Christ. For he is our peace, who has made us both one, and has broken down the dividing wall of hostility . . . that he . . . might reconcile us both to God in one body through the cross, thereby bringing the hostility to an end" (Ephesians 2:13-16, RSV).

Jesus and Walls

Jesus specialized in tearing down walls. He associated with sinners around whom the Pharisees had built a wall of isolation. He invited Himself to the home of Zacchaeus, the dishonest tax collector, around whom his fellow Jews had built a wall of hatred. He talked with the Samaritan woman at the well, thereby tearing down the wall behind which in His day women were segregated as inferior beings. He leveled the walls between the Jews and Samaritans, the Gentile and the Jew, the slave and the free. Jesus was the only teacher tall enough to look over the fences that divided the human race into compartments. St. Paul writes in the Epistle lesson today, "There is neither Jew nor Greek, (the dividing wall of nation and race); there is neither slave nor free, (the wall of class hatred); there is neither male nor female, (the barrier of sex); for you are all one in Christ Jesus" (Galatians 3:28).

Jesus: A Bridge-Builder

It's always a great day when a new bridge is dedicated. People on both sides of the structure rejoice because they are able to REACH each other easier and faster. They are glad because they conquered with their new bridge the space that separated them.

We are proud of our great bridges. They are really sights to behold. The George Washington Bridge between New York and New Jersey, the Golden Gate Bridge in California, and many others are engineering marvels of both beauty and utility.

But building bridges is not the business of civil engineers and construction workers alone. It is everyone's business. As Jesus built a bridge to come to us, so He wants us to be bridge builders. Much of our happiness, harmony, and success depends upon how well we build "human" bridges.

We have seen what the infamous Berlin Wall has done in terms of international relations. It has come to be a symbol of suffering, separation, and sickness. Yet, often in our own personal relations we build walls just as despicable as the one which divides East and West Berlin.

Jesus is not a wall; He is a bridge. By nature we are builders of walls; we live defensively; we erect fortresses; we dig moats; we hold people off. But Jesus is a bridge; He built the greatest bridge of all: that between God and man. "But now in Christ Jesus you who were once far off have been brought near in the blood of Christ" (Eph. 2:13).

How do we build bridges? The construction engineer builds them with steel and concrete. As "human engineers", we build them with the strong cables of kindness and courtesy. We build them with the solid girders of love and forgiveness. We reach people by paving the roadway of our bridge with patience and praise.

We build our bridge to God by repentence and forgiveness. To confess our sins to God is not to tell Him anything He doesn't already know. Until we confess them, however, they are a wall between God and us. Once we confess them, they become a bridge.

Man's Great Unfinished Task

Man has broken down many walls in recent years. He has broken the wall in the atom releasing its vast energy. He has broken the sound barrier and can now travel faster than sound. He has broken the barrier to outer space. But he has yet to tear down the greatest of all walls: the one separating man from man.

As Jesus broke down "the dividing wall of hostility" between man and God, so He gives us power today through faith, through prayer, through the Holy Spirit, through the Sacraments, through love and forgiveness to tear down the dividing walls of hostility that exist in our hearts, in our families, in our cities, in the world.

"Something there is that doesn't love a wall, that wants it down," said Robert Frost.

We would say, "*Someone* there is who doesn't love a wall."

That someone is Christ. That someone should be every follower of Christ.

PRAYER

Lord, forgive us the walls we have so thoughtlessly built, shutting ourselves off from others and forcing us to live lives all too lonely. Give us the faith and strength to bridge the space that would so cruelly separate us from those about us. Amen.

"I Have Already Died"

Eleventh Sunday of Luke (Colossians 3:4-11)

"Put to death therefore what is earthly in you: immorality, impurity, passion, evil desire, and covetousness which is idolatry" (Col. 3:5).

A bishop was imprisoned in a German concentration camp during the Second World War. He was being tortured by an S.S. officer who sought to force him to a confession. In a small room the two men were facing each other, one afflicting the other with increasing pain. The bishop, who had a remarkable tolerance for pain, did not respond to the torture. This enraged the officer who began to hit him harder until he finally exploded and shouted at him, "But don't you know that I can kill you?" The bishop looked in the eyes of his torturer and said slowly, "Yes, I know—do what you want—but I have already died." At that moment the S.S. officer realized that he was powerless over his victim who did not fear the most terrible thing he could do to him.

I Have Already Died

"I have already died." To see what these words mean we must turn to today's epistle lesson where we hear St. Paul saying:

"Put to death therefore what is earthly in you: immorality,

impurity, passion, evil desire, and covetousness, which is idolatry. On account of these the wrath of God is coming. In these you once walked, when you lived in them. But now you put them away: anger, wrath, malice, slander, and foul talk from your mouth. Do not lie to one another, seeing that you have put off the old nature with its practices and have put on the new nature, which is being renewed in knowledge after the image of its creator" (Col. 3:5-10).

We are to put to death what is earthly in us since we have put off the old Adam nature and have put on the new Christ nature. "I have already died."

Just before St. Paul lists the various qualities that are "the fruit of the Spirit," he speaks of the enemies of the Spirit that are to be crucified:

"Now the works of the flesh are plain: immorality, impurity, licentiousness, idolatry, sorcery, enmity, strife, jealousy, anger, selfishness, dissension, party spirit, envy, drunkenness, carousing, and the like. I warn you as I warned you before, that those who do such things shall not inherit the kingdom of God" (Gal. 5:19-21).

These are "the works of the flesh," the enemies of the Spirit, that are to be put to death in us. "And those who belong to Christ Jesus have crucified the flesh with its passions and desires" (Gal. 5:24). "*I have already died.*"

Let the New Nature Rise

We die to the old nature that the new nature might rise. Listen to Paul's description of the new nature:

"But the fruit of the Spirit is love, joy, peace, patience, kindness, goodness, faithfulness, gentleness, self-control; against such there is no law" (Gal. 5:22, 23).

It is from the death of the old that the new must rise. To find life we must first die to life as we know it. To find meaning we must first die to meaning as we know it. This is why St.

Paul says, "I die every day" (I Cor. 15:31).

Every day the Christian renounces the supremacy of his own will. Every day he renews his unconditional surrender to Christ as Lord. "I die every day."

Every day we are called to die to unbelief, to complacency, to mediocrity; to die to our discouragements, to our fears, our uncertainties, our suspicions that we may rise to confidence, trust, relinquishment, love, courage, generosity and hope. "I die every day" to the old nature that I may rise with Christ a new person.

Living Is a Matter of Life and Death

Living is a matter of life and death. As we go through life we die and live again many times. The infant dies for the child to live. The child dies to make way for the teenager. The teenager dies so the adult can emerge. And so into old age, we go constantly from life to death and death into life. "I die every day."

Part of me is dying every moment. Moment by moment cells in my body are dying and being replaced with new ones. If this didn't happen, I wouldn't be alive. "I die every day."

Medical science tells us that the body dies a little every day. Aging is a gentle decline that begins around the 30th birthday. Slowly, gradually, the body begins to die. "I die every day."

"Little Deaths"

So it is that my life in Christ is filled with "little deaths." My claim to comfort must die when I am faced with another's hurt. My right to justice must be given up when there is someone who needs mercy. My right to indulge myself must go when I am faced with a person who is dying of starvation. "I die every day."

"Consider yourselves dead to sin and alive to God in Christ Jesus," says Paul in Romans. Paul did not spend his life burying that dead man who died on the road to Damascus. He boldly turned his back on him once and for all in order that the life of Christ in him might have room for growth and ultimate glory. "For you have died, and your life is hid with Christ in God. When Christ Who is our life appears, then you also will appear with him in glory" (Col. 3:3-4).

"As dying and behold we live" says Paul. This voluntary death to what is earthly and sinful in us is the means given us by God to obtain eternal life. Die and you will live. If you don't want to die to what is earthly in you, then you are already dead. "I die every day."

The Way to Peace

An older Christian was asked by a younger person if he had "found peace." He answered, "No, dear friend, not peace but constant struggle." In a sense the Christian life is a constant struggle. It demands continuous warfare against the enemies of that life. "Put to death what is earthly in you."

One of the desert fathers says that when someone claims, "I have died to the world," he should be reminded, "Don't be so confident, brother, until you depart from the body. You may say, 'I have died'; but Satan has not died."

When Socrates faced death without fear but rather with a spirit of gaiety, he explained that true philosophers "are always occupied in the practice of dying." By this he meant the process by which we become progressively liberated from the compulsions of the flesh. Such daily dying might better be called "Operation Liberation." "The saying is sure: If we die with him, we shall also live with him" (II Tim. 2:11-13).

George Muller said once, "There was a day when I died; utterly died; died to George Muller, his opinions, preferences, tastes and will; died to the world, its approval or censure; died to the approval or blame even of my brethren and friends and, since then, I have studied only to show myself approved unto God."

Three Kinds of Death

There are three kinds of death:

1. I have died with Christ in baptism. "Do you not know that all of us who have been baptized into Christ Jesus were baptized into his death? We were buried therefore with him by baptism into death, so that as Christ was raised from the dead by the glory of the Father, we too might walk in newness of life" (Romans 6:3-4). I have died with Christ in baptism. My sins were drowned and I rose to a new life.

2. I am dying with Christ every day to what is earthly and sinful in me.

3. I will die one day a physical death.

But if I have died the first two deaths (in baptism and to what is earthly in me), then the third death (the physical one) will not be a death but a resurrection. Operation liberation! Thus it was that the bishop who had already died the first two deaths, did not fear the third death at the hands of the S.S. officer.

PRAYER

Lord, help me to prepare for physical death
by dying daily—dying to the failures of the past,
dying to the limitations of the present,
dying to what is earthly and sinful in me.
For to die this way is to live,
to release myself to new possibilities in life,
to let the new nature of Christ within me
grow more and more like unto the perfect image:
Christ. Amen.

What To Do With Anger

Twelfth Sunday of Luke (Colossians 3:4-11)

"But now put . . . away . . . anger" (Col. 3:8).

St. Paul calls on us in the Epistle lesson today to put to death what is earthly in us. One of the things he urges us to remove from our lives is anger. "But now put . . . away . . . anger" (Col. 3:8).

Yet elsewhere in his epistles Paul does not condemn anger. He writes, for example, in Ephesians 4:26, "Be angry but do not sin; do not let the sun go down on your anger, and give no opportunity to the devil." J. B. Phillips paraphrases the passage this way: "If you are angry, be sure it is not out of wounded pride or bad temper. Never go to bed angry—don't give the devil that sort of foothold."

First Paul says, "Put . . . away . . . anger." Then he says "Be angry but do not sin." The two verses have puzzled many people. They seem contradictory, but in reality they are not. Anger has a definite place in the Christian's life. In fact, the lack of it can even be an indication of spiritual weakness.

Aristotle said once: "Anybody can become angry—that is easy; but to be angry with the right person, and to the right degree, and at the right time, and in the right way—that is not within everybody's power, and is not easy." Anger can be good or bad depending on what we do with it. There are times when it can be a great virtue. There are times when it needs to be "put away."

When Anger Is Sinful

Anger becomes sinful when we are angry for the wrong reason, at the wrong person, at the wrong time, and in the wrong way. It is when we become angry because of wounded pride or bad temper, or because of personal pique or envy that anger becomes sinful. Such anger is always destructive.

We are to put away the kind of anger that is a boiling passion within us; the kind of anger that is abiding and habitual; the kind of anger that cannot forget a hurt or an injury; the kind of anger that nurses its wrath to keep it warm; the kind of anger that seeks revenge. This is uncontrolled anger; anger that is sinful.

Brief Madness

The ancient Greeks were not far wrong when they defined anger as a "brief madness." When a man is angry, he is not in control of himself. That is why we use the expression "he lost his temper." An angry person loses more than his temper; he loses total control over himself. Any person who can make his opponent lose his temper has already defeated him. Ghandi said once, "When you are in the right, you can afford to keep your temper, and when you are in the wrong, you can't afford to lose it." A person once said of a mountain: "This would have been our tallest mountain if it hadn't blown its top." This can be said of many people who could not control their anger. One fellow claims he never loses his temper. But he admits, "Occasionally I do mislay it." Whether it is lost or mislaid, anger becomes sinful and destructive when we cannot keep it under control. "Speak when you are angry," someone said, "and you will make the best speech you will ever regret."

Misdirected Anger

Anger becomes sinful when it is misdirected; when we take

it off on the wrong person. The real tragedy of anger is that its victims are so often not the ones who caused it. How many auto accidents occur because we happen to be angry with someone, and we take it off on the car or on the other driver! The worker who gets angry with his boss, goes home and lashes out at his wife or kids. How often our load of anger is dumped onto someone who doesn't deserve it at all? The sin of anger is that it spreads like an infection. One angry person makes two or three more people angry.

An alert bus driver shot this friendly question at a man who was grouchy with him and his fellow passengers:

"Did you quarrel with your wife this morning?"

"Yes," the man admitted with surprise.

"That's your private affair," said the driver and quietly remarked, "why make it public?"

The trouble with anger is that if it is not expressed honestly and in love toward the one to whom it is directed, it will go public; it will be misdirected to hurt innocent people.

Don't Pretend

Anger becomes sinful, says St. Paul, when "we let the sun go down" on it (Eph. 4:26). That is, when we do not express it properly; when we let it fester within. Paul urges us to get anger out into the open and deal with it. A person who simply pretends not to be angry, pushing it down inside, does exactly what the Bible says we should *not* do. He lets the sun go down on his anger, and he gives a mighty foothold to the devil.

Elsewhere St. Paul says, "Be angry but do not sin." "Be angry" he says. In other words, accept anger as a valid emotion. Don't pretend it isn't there. Don't try to suppress it. Admit it. Anger is energy. Once provoked it has to find an outlet somewhere. If it does not come out in an acceptable way, it will come out in an unacceptable way.

For example, a husband gets angry with his wife. He may feel, however, it's bad to express anger in marriage because it destroys love. Perhaps he feels that he shouldn't even have any anger toward his wife. But this energy has to come out somewhere. So what does he do? Instead of being honest with his wife and telling her in love that he is angry and why he is angry, he begins to criticize her cooking and to find fault with her in many different ways to the point where the wife wonders what's wrong with him. What's wrong is that instead of expressing his anger directly to his wife so that she knows what's hurting him, he's letting it come out indirectly in many subtle ways that are destroying love and making life miserable. This would not happen if we were honest about our anger.

William Blake had some advice for the angry heart. He wrote,

"I was angry with my friend:
I told my wrath, my wrath did end.
I was angry with my foe:
I hid my wrath, my wrath did grow."

Anger always grows when it is not expressed. It broods over hurts; it harbors suspicions and grudges; it slowly poisons one's outlook killing the joy of life. The antidote—telling your wrath—releases the poison, restores communication and brings understanding. But everything depends on *how* we "tell our wrath." We can "blow our top," in which case we can really hurt the other person, or we can "tell our wrath" in love. There is a great difference between the two.

When Anger Is Not Sinful

Victor Hugo said once, "Pride robs me of God, envy of my neighbor, and anger of myself." But there is such a thing as *just anger.* Not all anger is sinful. When anger is controlled; when its energy is directed to eradicating the evils in my life; when it is anger "with the right person, to the right degree, at the right time, for the right purpose, and in the right way," then it can become a tool for growth and change.

Anger can be directed and used constructively; in fact,

there is great creative power in anger, especially if it is spiritually dedicated.

Abraham Lincoln once saw a black family being auctioned off to various bidders. As a young man he was filled with such anger as to say, "If I ever get a chance to strike a death blow at this travesty on human justice, I will do it, no matter what it costs." It cost him and the nation dearly, but when he became President he issued the Emancipation Proclamation.

Somebody ought to get angry at the injustices in our world today. If literally nothing angers us as Christians, we may well question the validity of our faith.

Anger is a God-given emotion meant to be directed against sin and injustice. The adrenalin it releases in the blood stream almost triples our energy. It is reserve power to jar us out of inertia, to inflame us with zeal for the things that are good and true. A pastor said once, "Ordinarily I weigh 120 pounds. But when I am angry I weigh a ton." If today we have humane mental hospitals, it is because of an angry Dorothy Dix who long ago battled against the inhumanities practiced in such hospitals. If we have pure food laws on our books today, it is because someone became angry. If there are still many injustices in society today, it is because we do not feel a sense of outrage anymore.

St. Chrysostom on Anger

Speaking on anger St. John Chrysostom said, "We have anger given us, not that we may commit acts of violence on our neighbors, but that we may correct those that are in sin, that we may bestir ourselves, that we may not be sluggish. Anger is implanted in us as a sort of sting, to make us gnash with our teeth against the devil, to make us vehement against him, not to set us . . . against each other. . . . Are you prone to anger? Be so against your own sins: chastise your soul, scourge your conscience, be a severe judge, and merciless in your sentence against your own sins. This is the way to turn anger to account. It was for that that God implanted anger within us."

The trouble with most of us is that we become angry with trifles. We are dressing in a hurry and our shoelace breaks. Or we miss a green light because of a slow driver in front of us. These things make us angry, but about the injustices and sins in our lives and in society we feel little or no anger. "The size of a man can be measured by the size of the thing that makes him angry." Sometimes we spend $1,000.00 worth of emotion to get rid of a five-cent irritation.

How to Deal With Anger

1. One of the ways to dissipate anger is through forgiveness. When Leonardo da Vinci was working on his painting "The Last Supper," he became angry with a certain man. Losing his temper he lashed out at him with bitter words and threats. Returning to his canvas he attempted to work on the face of Jesus, but was unable to do so. He was so upset he could not compose himself for the painstaking work. Finally he put down his tools, sought out the man, and asked his forgiveness. The man accepted his apology and Leonardo was able to return to his workshop and finish painting the face of Jesus. Forgiveness is one of the best remedies for anger.

2. Dr. Haim Ginott said something about anger that applies equally to children and parents: "Anger should so come out that it brings some relief to the parents, some insight to the child, and no harmful effects to either."

3. Another healthy outlet for anger is sports, long brisk walks, push-ups, golf, jogging, tennis, bowling. These are excellent releases for anger and hostility. Adequate periods of play and rest are also vital.

One person said, "One Saturday morning I awoke early, got out my push lawn mower and tackled every blade of grass in my yard." "Were you angry?" his wife asked. "Yes, I was," he answered, "and I used it to get my lawn mowed."

Dr. Karl Meninger, eminent psychiatrist, wrote, "Instead of a fist fight, a tennis game; instead of a foray against a person, a crop of weeds vehemently attacked. Such transformations . . . of the aggressive energies are occuring constantly in everyday life."

4. Seneca said once that the greatest cure for anger is delay. If you think it silly to count to ten, then start praying the Lord's Prayer.

5. Next time you feel the surge of anger, say to yourself, "Is it really worth what it's going to do to me and others emotionally? I will make a fool of myself. I may hurt someone I love, or I might lose a friend." Is it worth it for me to lose my temper and have to pay such a price?

6. Try to express your anger before you reach the boiling point.

7. Admit that you are angry. Recognize the feelings and uncover them.

8. Accept the fact that it's perfectly normal to get angry, especially at people closest to you. It's the way you express anger that makes the difference.

9. Pinpoint what has made you angry. When we can locate the source, we have insight that will be of great help.

10. Learn to recognize your own internal anger signals.

11. Don't misdirect your anger. Express it at the real target whenever possible—but always in love.

12. When you can't express your anger publicly—for example, when you're at work—find a harmless way to release it.

13. Remember that many times the person you're really angry at is yourself.

14. Uncontrolled anger requires a loud voice. Keep your volume low. No one can get very angry in a whisper.

15. Seek forgiveness every day. Don't let minor irritations accumulate.

16. Seek to control and direct the energy of anger toward the destruction of evil and sin.

17. Open up all your hostile feelings to the presence of God through prayer and confession.

PRAYER

Precious Lord, Who can control and direct the emotion of anger without the power and presence of Your Holy Spirit within? Fill us with Your Spirit that we may transform this potentially destructive emotion into a tool for growth and change. Amen.

"Making the Most of Time"

Thirteenth Sunday of Luke (Ephesians 5:8-19)

"Look carefully then how you walk, not as unwise men but as wise, making the most of the time, because the days are evil" (Ephesians 5:15-16).

"I have only just a minute,
Only 60 seconds in it,
Forced upon me—can't refuse it,
Didn't seek it, didn't choose it,
But it's up to me to use it—
Give account if I abuse it;
Just a tiny little minute—
BUT ETERNITY IS IN IT."

Time is too precious a gift, too scarce a commodity to be squandered. If we waste it, we lose more opportunities than we know. Each moment is an opportunity for prayer, for kindness, for self-control, for personal growth. "Make the best possible use of your time," says Paul (Col. 4:5).

If time is charged with opportunity (kairos time in Greek), and not merely a succession of empty moments (chronos time in Greek), it is shameful to waste it and sinful to kill it. The Bible places the accent upon time as kairos, as a God-given opportunity for us to use, to repent, to turn to Jesus, to love God and neighbor, to grow more and more unto His likeness.

How we spend time is far more important than how we

spend money. Money mistakes can be corrected, but when time is gone, it is gone forever.

Give each of three people a suitcase of identicial size and usually one will succeed in filling the suitcase with far more articles than the other. Our days are all the same. But what a difference in the way we pack them!

How can we make the most of time? How can we make the best possible use of it?

Use Those Spare Moments

First, we must learn to use our spare moments.

John Erskine, the well-known author and lecturer, said that he learned the most valuable lesson of his life when he was 14 years of age. His piano teacher asked him how much he practiced each day. He replied that he usually sat down for an hour or more. "Oh, don't do that," warned the instructor. "When you grow up, time won't come to you in long stretches like that. Do your practicing in minutes whenever you can find them—5 or 10 before school, a few after lunch or in between chores. Spread it throughout the day, and music will become part of your life." Erskine said later that he applied this principle to his writing. He wrote nearly all of his most famous work, "The Private Life of Helen of Troy," on streetcars while commuting between his home and the university.

Some of the busiest people I know get the most reading done because they always have a book or magazine handy when there is an occasion to wait.

A man went to a barber shop one day and was astonished to find the barber able to speak perfect Spanish. "When did you learn to speak the language so well?" the man asked.

"Right here," said the barber. "I taught myself Spanish here in the shop between haircuts."

A Greek elevator maintenance man named Nicholas Christofilos was interested in modern science. Every day after work, before he sat down to his supper, he devoted an hour to reading books on nuclear physics. As he began to understand the subject more clearly, ideas came into his mind. In 1948 he set down a plan for a particle accelerator that he thought would be cheaper and more powerful than any in existence. He sent his plans to the U.S. Atomic Energy Commission for testing. It worked so well that it saved the United States some 70 million dollars. Christofilos received two awards: $10,000. in cash and a position at the University of California's Radiation Laboratory.

"Don't tell me you have no time for prayer," said a famous bishop." "Pray as you shine your shoes."

"Fill up each hour with what will last;
Buy up the moments as they go;
The life above, when this is past,
Is the ripe fruit of life below" (Bonar).

Do it Now!

Make the most of time first by using those spare moments, and secondly by not procrastinating, by doing it now.

When I have time, so many things I'll do
To make life happier and more fair
For those whose lives are crowded now with care;
I'll help to lift them from their low despair
When I have time.

When I have time the friend I love so well
Shall know no more these weary toiling days;
I'll lead her feet in pleasant paths always
And cheer her heart with words of sweetest praise
When I have time.

When you have time the friend you hold so dear
May be beyond the reach of all your sweet intent
May never know that you so kindly meant
To fill her life with sweet content
When you had time.

Now is the time. Ah, friend, no longer wait
To scatter loving smiles, and words of cheer;
They may not need you in the coming year
    Now is the time.

Today is all we have to work with. If we have anything important to do, do it now! The past is irretrievably gone, the future is not here. British art expert John Ruskin had the word "TODAY" carved into a small marble block that he kept on his desk as a constant reminder to "DO IT NOW." An anonymous philosopher said:

"Yesterday is a cancelled check.
Tomorrow is a promissory note.
Today is ready cash. Use it."

Planned Neglect

The third way of making the most of time in addition to using spare moments and doing it now, is what we shall call planned neglect.

A wise person conserves time through planned neglect. When asked the secret of her marvelous success with the violin, a young concert artist replied, "Planned neglect." She explained, "When I began the study of music, there were many things that always demanded my time. Going to my room after breakfast, I made my bed, dusted my room, arranged my things on the dresser, and did whatever else would make my room neat and attractive. After I had finished these tasks, I turned to my violin. I soon discovered that that system would keep me from forever becoming a good violinist. So I deliberately planned to neglect everything else each day until my practice period was completed."

Asked by a friend why—still young, and at the height of her fame—she had withdrawn from the operatic stage, Jenny Lind, the famous singer, answered as she picked up her Bible: "Because I found it left me so little time for this and"—pointing to the sunset—"none for that."

Planned neglect of the less important, conserves time for the more important things in life.

Establish a Priority

Make the most of time by using spare moments, by doing it now, by planned neglect, and lastly by establishing a priority system, putting first things first.

When Charles M. Schwab was president of Bethlehem Steel he said to Ivy Lee, a management consultant: "Show me a way to get more things done. If it works, I'll pay anything within reason."

Lee handed Schwab a piece of paper, "Write down the things you have to do tomorrow," he said. Schwab did it. "Now number these items in the order of their real importance," Lee said. Schwab complied. "The first thing tomorrow morning," Lee added, "start working on number one and stay with it until it is completed. Next take number two and don't go any further until it is completed. Then proceed to number three, and so on. If you can't complete anything on schedule, don't fret. At least you will have taken care of the most important things before getting distracted by items of lesser importance.

"The secret is to do this daily," continued Lee. "Evaluate the relative importance of things you have to get done . . . establish priorities . . . record your plan of action . . . and stick to it. Do this every working day."

In a few weeks Charles Schwab sent Ivy Lee a check for $25,000. Schwab said later that this lesson was the most profitable one he had ever learned in his business career.

What a difference it would make in our lives as disciples of Jesus if we established daily such a priority of things to be done in the order of their real importance based on the prayer: "Lord, what are the things You really want me to do today for You, for my family, for my business, for others, for myself?"

It is this kind of a priority system that Jesus urges us to establish when He says, "Seek first the kingdom of God and His righteousness and all these things will be added to you."

"It is not enough to be busy," said Thoreau, "so are the ants. The question is what are we busy about?" Jesus came to teach us the truly important things in life about which we ought to be busy. "Labor not for the food that perishes," He said, "Labor rather for the food that endures to life everlasting."

So if you want to make the best possible use of that most precious commodity of time, follow this fourfold plan: use those spare moments; if you have something important to do, don't procrastinate, do it now; plan to neglect unimportant things that are time sappers; establish the kind of priority system taught by Jesus putting first things first and tackling them one at a time.

When it comes to a commodity as precious as time we all need to become efficiency experts.

Goethe said, "The day is immeasurably long to him who knows not how to value and use it."

St. Paul put it this way: "Look carefully then how you walk, not as unwise men but as wise, making the most of the time, because the days are evil" (Ephesians 5:15-16).

PRAYER

Dear Lord, time—our years on earth—fleeting as they are—are the stuff of which eternity is made. Help us to use them to gain the great gift of life with You. Amen.

The Foremost of Sinners

Fourteenth Sunday of Luke (1 Timothy 1:15-17)

"The saying is sure and worthy of full acceptance, that Christ Jesus came into the world to save sinners. And I am the foremost of sinners; but I received mercy for this reason, that in me, as the foremost, Jesus Christ might display his perfect patience for an example to those who were to believe in him for eternal life" (I Timothy 1:15-16).

President Coolidge never wasted words. One Sunday he returned to the White House after attending church alone. "Was the sermon good?" his wife asked. "Yes," he answered. "What was it about?" "Sin." "What did the minister say?" "He was against it."

In today's Epistle lesson the Apostle Paul certainly has more to say about sin than Coolidge had.

Man today tries to evade the issue of sin—so much so that the word "sin" is hardly ever used any more. In fact, a distinguished Christian psychiatrist, Dr. Karl Meninger, wrote a book, whose title asks the question: "Whatever Became of Sin?"

What did become of sin?

Sensitivity to Sin

A person once separated two men who were fighting.

"What's this all about?" he asked. "I called him a liar," growled one. "Suppose I am a liar!" roared the other. "I've got a right to be sensitive about it, haven't I?"

Aren't we all sensitive about our sins? There was a man once who was so proud of his accomplishments that he decided to look into his family tree to discover the reason for his greatness. He stumbled upon some very disgraceful information concerning a certain Uncle Josh, who had been in prison and had been electrocuted. But he was so sensitive about it that when he wrote the account in his family archives, he glossed over it with fancy language: "Uncle Josh occupied the chair of applied electricity in one of our leading government institutions. He was attached to this position by the strongest of ties; and his death came as a great shock."

Does being sensitive about sin and glossing over it with fine words make it go away? We have had a half century of "sinless" society, but are we free from guilt? Modern man doesn't worry much about sin any more. He has conveniently pushed it under the rug. He worries instead about all the consequences of sin: guilt, despair, low-esteem, etc. As long as sin remains under the rug; as long as it is not brought to God in humble and tearful repentance, the consequences of sin will continue to make life miserable for man.

Loss of Sense of Sin

Perhaps the greatest sin in the world today is that people have begun to lose their sense of sin. For example, the old sin of adultery is now seen as a means to personal fulfillment—an expression of freedom and love—and therefore not at all a sin but a virtue. The old sin of homosexuality is seen today as being simply a different life style. And if it's not virtuous, at least it's not immoral. It's only different. Lest we begin feeling better than others at this point, let it be said that while the practice of homosexuality is a sin, so is the attitude that looks upon the sins of others as worse than our own. Not one of us is without sin. Not one of us can point the finger at another. Only Christ can. Yet instead of pointing the finger, Christ stretched out His arms upon the cross in forgiveness. "Christ Jesus came into the world to save sinners."

Sin Blinds

"If we say we have no sin, we deceive ourselves, and the truth is not in us" (I John 1:8). Yet we do say we have no sin—many of us. It is easy to fool ourselves because as Aristotle said, the easiest person in the world to deceive is oneself. Sin is dangerous and deceptive precisely because it is so blind to itself. It calls "evil good and good evil." It puts "darkness for light and light for darkness." It puts "bitter for sweet and sweet for bitter" (Isaiah 5:20).

It belongs to the nature of sin to blind as it grows; the more you have of it, the less you see of it. That is why people who do not believe in God and ignore His church are always the first to protest that they are not sinners. They find the words of St. Paul in today's Epistle lesson most distasteful, " . . . Christ Jesus came into the world to save sinners. And I am the foremost of sinners . . . " (I Tim. 1:15). It is the nature of sin to blind us to itself. As William Temple said, "No crime looks so bad to the man who has committed it as to the man who has kept clear of it. As soon as we have done something that is nasty, we have blunted our own capacity to be disgusted, we have tarnished the mirror in which we are to look at our own reflection." Yet the experts who are being quoted today are the great sinners. The movie actress is quoted in the magazine as an authority on men. After all, she's had seven husbands. The wealthy sportsman is quoted in the newspaper concerning automobiles. He's an authority—having had seven wrecks. But the poor amateurs who have never failed in marriage, or wrecked a car, what do they know! Thus, it comes to pass, as Jesus said, that the blind become leaders of the blind.

Whence the Awareness of Sin?

Why is it that St. Paul had such a great awareness of sin that he called himself "the foremost of sinners," whereas many people today have no awareness of sin? The answer is that our sense of sin is in proportion to our nearness to God. The closer we are to Him, the greater will be our awareness of how much we have failed Him and ourselves. The farther we are from Him the less will be the awareness of sin. Fr. Danielou expressed it well when he said, "It is the saints who have a sense of sin. The sense of sin is a measure of the soul's awareness of God." It was because of Paul's closeness to Christ that he was able to see himself as "the foremost of sinners."

It was when Isaiah was ushered into the very presence of God in a vision and saw the Lord sitting on a throne, high and lifted up, that he realized his sinfulness: "Woe is me! For I am lost, for I am a man of unclean lips, for my eyes have seen the king, the Lord of hosts." It was when the Apostle Peter had a special awareness of who Jesus was that he said, "Depart from me for I am a sinful man, O Lord." Awareness of sin is always related to our closeness to God.

Metropolitan Anthony Bloom once said in an interview:

"The realm of God is a dangerous one. To meet God is to enter the cave of a tiger. God is the true measure of our greatness. Whenever we find ourselves face to face with God, we have entered the realm of judgement. Either we are found wanting or else we are found moving toward fulfillment. God's judgement doesn't mean condemnation; it means appraisal, and it means challenge. On the one hand, God is our peace. God is our reconciliation. God is life—abundance of life. On the other hand, God is never satisfied with less than ourselves truly fulfilled. In the eyes of God, nothing but fullness and abundance is good enough for us."

A young cynic once said to a preacher, "You talk about the burden of sin. I feel none. How heavy is it? Fifty pounds?

Ten pounds? The preacher answered, "Tell me, if you laid four hundred pounds of weight on a corpse, would it feel the load?" "No, because it is dead," replied the youth. "So it is when one is dead to God. He doesn't feel the weight of sin."

What Is Sin?

What is sin? Sin is the separation of man from himself, from his fellow humans, and from God. As Tillich said, "We know we are separated from something to which we really belong; something with which we should be united." Because it separates us from God, and others, sin builds walls and makes us depressingly lonely. Sin is not merely the breaking of a list of rules; it is a power that possesses man. It dwells in us, controls us, makes us do what we don't want to do. Sin is doing nothing when I should be doing something. Sin is the priest and the levite rushing by the wounded man on the road to Jericho and doing nothing to help because they didn't want to be late for their appointment with God in the Temple. "Whoever knows what is right to do and fails to do it, for him it is sin" (James 4:17). Sin in Greek (amartia) means failure to hit the bull's eye; failure to be what God created us to be. Sin is failure to treat our fellow humans as human beings created in the image of God. Sin is hybris, pride, making oneself instead of God, the center of the universe. Sin is refusing to let God love us. Sin is anything that creates distance between God and man. If you keep all the commandments and disobey just one, you have sinned. "It is no great matter," said Cardinal Newman, "that we obey the Master in the 99 cases where to do so is easy. The real test for us lies in the 100th case where it is hard." Sin is not realizing that the extra coat in the closet belongs to him who shivers out in the cold because he has none; the extra loaf of bread in our pantry belongs to him who is dying of starvation in Bangladesh. Sin is what makes me put my own desires before everything else. It's what makes me lack pity for others; it's what takes away my courage in the face of difficulties; it's what makes me lose my faith in God;

it's what makes me envy even those I love; it's what keeps my tongue tied when just a word is needed to heal; it's what makes me give excuses for not doing acts of mercy and love; it's what keeps me from spending more time with God in prayer; it's what clouds the vision of God for us and makes us afraid of the light. Plato said once, "We can easily forgive a child who is afraid of the dark; the real tragedy of life is when men are afraid of the light." Sin is murder—not just physical murder but all the other kinds of murder. Who hasn't killed a hope or crushed an expectation? Doesn't a sneer, a contemptuous look, a biting word often strike at the heart of a person like a poisoned arrow? Is not this, too, murder? We talk about big sins and little sins, supposing that the "big" sins are what really matter while the "little" ones—a white lie, an angry word, an offensive remark—are all right. But here we must remember an Indian proverb which says, "There is no distinction between big and little when talking about snakes. They are all alike—snakes." Sin is not merely the breaking of a law; it is the breaking of a personal relationship with God, the breaking of God's heart, the breaking of His Body on the Cross. When we see the supreme sacrifice Christ offered on the Cross to forgive us, we begin to realize that sin is so serious as to require the crucifixion of God. If all this is what sin is, then I have sinned against God many, many times. How can I, too, not say with St. Paul, "I am the foremost of sinners"?

Many Sins—One Cure

When a preacher announced that there were 726 sins, he was beseiged for copies of the list. There are many sins, many ways of disobeying God, of sinning. Chesterton said once, "It is always simple to fall, there are an infinity of angles at which one falls, only one at which one stands."

The only way to stand is with Christ. Paul does not let the confession that he is "the foremost of sinners" stand alone. He connects it immediately to Christ: "Christ Jesus came into the world to save sinners . . . I received mercy for this reason, that in me, Jesus Christ might display his perfect patience for an example to those who were to believe in him for eternal life" (I Tim. 1:15-16). If Christ could forgive me, the foremost of sinners, says Paul, then He certainly can forgive anyone else.

A sense of sin can lead either to despair or to God. Paul says that it is meant to lead us to God; to the forgiveness, peace and new life that only He can give.

There is something bigger than sin—and that is God's grace. "Where sin abounded, grace did much more abound" (Rom. 5:20). God's grace is always greater than any sin. That is why Paul emphasizes, "The saying is *sure* and *worthy of full acceptance*, that Christ Jesus came into the world to save sinners" (I Tim. 1:15). Mark these words "sure" and "worthy of full acceptance."

After a young preacher had delivered one of his first sermons, an older preacher said to him kindly, "You made sin so big and God so little! Had I not known better I would have left the church feeling that sin was bigger and stronger than God."

We want no one ever to leave church with that kind of a false impression which is a complete denial of the Gospel of Jesus. "Greater is he that is in you (God), than he that is in the world (the devil)" (I John 4:4).

When there is garbage in the house, a deodorizer will simply not do. The garbage has to be removed. The most efficient garbage collector in the universe is the Savior. "Christ Jesus came into the world to save sinners" (I Tim. 1:15).

If Christianity talks much about sin, it is because it alone has the cure for sin. "I came into the world not to call the righteous but sinners to repentance," said Jesus. A doctor was once asked how he could endure being in the presence of so much disease with all its pain and suffering. He replied, "I always look at disease from the curative standpoint." We Christians always look at sin from the curative standpoint.

The first sermon Jesus ever preached dealt with the cure for sin: "Repent!" Make an about face, a U-turn. Return to the God Whom you have left; Whom your sin has crucified. He will forgive you, and accept you, and give you the power to become a new person in Christ.

PRAYER

I believe Lord, and confess that You are truly the Christ, the Son of the Living God, Who came into the world to save sinners, of whom I am the foremost. For me You came. For me You were crucified. For me You were resurrected that I may have forgiveness and life eternal with You. To You be all glory, honor and worship now and ever and unto ages of ages. Amen.

Saved By Hope

Fifteenth Sunday of Luke (I Timothy 4:9-15)

". . . we have set our hope on the living God . . ." (I Tim. 4:10)

You may recall the story of Pandora's box in Greek mythology. The gods presented Pandora with a box into which each had placed some evil. They forbade her ever to open it. One day in a moment of weakness she lifted the lid. To her horror out flew all the plagues, sorrows, and mischiefs which torment mankind. Pandora slammed the lid, but it was too late. Evil had been let loose in the world. One valuable thing, however, remained in the box: hope. It was the only good that remained with man and, according to this myth, to this day it is man's sole comfort in misfortune.

Prisoners of Hope

Have we ever stopped to think how important hope is in life? It would be unthinkable to live without it: hope for our children; hope for economic betterment; hope for better health; hope for success and advancement in our work. It is hope that keeps us going. As the prophet Zachariah put it, we are "prisoners of hope."

Whatever man does he does in hope. The farmer would never sow a seed in the soil, or the preacher preach a sermon, a mother undergo the pain of childbirth, a student the discipline of study, or a surgeon perform an operation, were it not for the hope that out of the effort something good, something better might result. The person who utterly loses hope in life is one who is likely to commit suicide. Ironically, even his suicide is done in hope, in hope that death is better than life. Man must hope! As Dr. Karl Menninger says, "Man can't help hoping, even if he is a scientist; he can only hope more accurately." Or as Mary Martin used to sing in "South Pacific," "I'm stuck like a dope with a thing called hope, and I can't get it out of my heart."

Looking at soldiers headed for war, an Air Force Chaplain said, "Hope is what they want." A medical doctor says of critically ill patients in his care, "Hope is what they need." An attendant says of patients in a large mental hospital, "Hope is what they've lost." "Hope is the anchor of the soul!" (Hebrews 6:19).

Saved By Hope

Man cannot exist without hope. Dr. Viktor Frankl who survived the Nazi concentration camps says that the most important factor in staying alive was hope. He saw hundreds of inmates die simply because they had given up hope. Those who survived, survived as they clung to hope. "For we are saved by hope" writes St. Paul (Romans 8:24).

Without food man can survive for close to thirty days; without water for little more than three days; without air hardly more than three minutes; but without hope he might destroy himself in an even shorter time. Nothing can nourish and sustain the soul of man as much as hope. Experiments have shown that even the lowly rats when placed in situations which seemed to permit no chance of escape, gave up their efforts for survival and rapidly succumbed to death—a death caused by loss of hope. Doctors tell us that loss of hope hastens the arrival of death in patients. What every patient needs most and what he receives least of—is hope. No person has the right ever to deprive another person of hope. It is said that where there is life there is hope. But the opposite is even more true: where there is hope there is life. Emil Brunner, the theologian, has written, "What oxygen is for the human lungs, such is hope for the meaning of human life . . . as the fate of the human is dependent on the supply of oxygen, so the fate of humanity is dependent on its supply of hope."

The Dynamic of Hope

Hope inspires dynamic effort. Behind the surging demands for civil rights, behind the young nations struggling to their feet in Africa, even behind the appeal of Communism is the dynamic of hope; hope that in the darkness of poverty and hunger and injustice a door will open that will lead to a better tomorrow.

Dr. John Stehlin, cancer specialist from Houston, Texas, observed that hope is the essence of our aliveness as human beings. He said, "There is an enormous difference between incurability and hopelessness. A person may be physically alive, but if he has given up hope, then, to me, he is a dead patient. Hopelessness is death." Dr. Stehlin will not allow the word hopeless to be used with his patients. "Physicians have used the words 'hopeless' and 'incurable' interchangeably," he said, "but no patient is ever hopeless. His physical condition may be incurable, but he is not hopeless. Hopelessness is a state of mind. It's a giving up. A pit of nothingness."

A Mood of Hopelessness

We speak of hope today because we live in a world where despair seems to have become the fashion. This mood of hopelessness was started by European existentialists. If anyone stands up and says that man was not made to live in a permanent anxiety neurosis he is quickly accused of being a shallow optimist, unacquainted with the cares and troubles of life.

Nietzsche said, "Hope is the worst of evils, for it prolongs the torment of man." But we Christians will forever stand up against this mood of despair. No true Christian can ever be a pessimist. On the contrary, he is an optimist—the greatest and the most incurable optimist in the world. Christian optimism is not based on shallow wish or false hope; it is based on God and what He in the Person of Christ has done—and can do for man—the God Whose forgiving love annihilates sin; the God Whose death on the cross destroyed the power of death. "In the world you have tribulation," said Jesus, "but be of good cheer, I have overcome the world."

"We have our hope set on the living God, Who is the Savior of all men, especially of those who believe" (I Tim. 4:10).

Our Only Hope

There is the story of the man who was on a sinking ship. The vessel was breaking up. The lifeboats had been torn away. The radio was not working. The passengers rushed to the ship's captian and asked: "Is there any way out?" The captain replied, "We've tried everything we can. Our only hope now is in God." The passengers were stunned. "Is it that bad?" one asked in disbelief. Far from being bad, what better hope can man ever have than that which is anchored in God. If man is without hope today, it is because he lives as if God were dead. St. Paul expressed it well when he described the unbelievers as *"Having no hope, and without God in the world."* To be without God—he says—is to be without hope. It has been said that the most profane word one can use is the word "hopeless." When one says that a situation or a person is hopeless, one is slamming the door in the face of God.

Our hopes with regard to earthly needs and desires are both natural and legitimate. Everyone should hope—and work—for better health, success in one's business or profession. But there is a higher, an eternal hope, a hope which alone gives meaning and direction in our life. And that is the hope in God Who "so loved the world that he gave his only begotten Son that whoever believes in him may not perish but have everlasting life" (John 3:16). If there were no God, if God were uninterested in the world He has made, Jesus would not have come. But He did come! And because He came there is hope. If there were no repentance or forgiveness, life would hold no hope for any of us. If death marked the end of man, life would indeed be a "tale told by an idiot." But in Jesus we have forgiveness and life. He is our hope, our joyful hope.

"The people who walked in darkness have seen a great light; those who dwelt in a land of deep darkness, on them has light shined." The great light that has shone to those who walk in darkness is Jesus. "For God sent not his Son into the world to condemn the world; but that the world through Him might be saved." He is our hope.

The Christian is never without hope, because he doesn't feel that he is imprisoned in a hall of anxiety from which there is no way out. He has found the way out in Christ. He knows that all things—even suffering and evil, can work for good to those who love God and cooperate with Him. He knows that there is nothing in all creation—not even death—that can separate him from the love of God in Christ Jesus. He knows that the sufferings of the present time are not worthy to be compared with the glory that shall be revealed to those who put their trust in Jesus.

This same note of hope is sounded throughout the Gospels: "Come, come," says God to man, "Come to the banquet for all is now ready." Elsewhere He says, "Come and drink of the water of life freely. . . . Come to me all you who labor and are heavy laden, and I will give you rest. . . . Come and inherit the kingdom prepared for you from the foundation of the world."

"Come you disconsolate, wherever you may languish. Come to the mercy seat, fervently kneel. Here bring your wounded hearts, here tell your anguish; earth has no sorrow that heaven cannot heal." This is our hope.

A People with Hope

St. Paul tells us that Christians are a people with hope. "You sorrow not as others who have no hope" (I Thess. 4:13). The Scriptures, he says, were "written for our instruction, that . . . by the encouragement of the Scriptures we might have hope" (Romans 15:4). Christ came to bring us the good news of hope. He offered us a hopeful view of God, a hopeful view of man and a hopeful view of history which would culminate in His Second Coming.

A father wept unashamedly. His heart was breaking as he helplessly stood by, watching his son waste a promising life with drugs. In an effort to comfort the father, a friend sympathized, "I guess you feel pretty hopeless." He looked up with a start. "No," he answered firmly. "*Hopelessness is unbelief* . . . it's atheistic. I believe in God. He will bring us through this!"

There are no hopeless situations in life; there are only people who have grown hopeless about them. And there can never be any such thing as a hopeless Christian. Someone said, "Suffering colors all of life, doesn't it?" "Yes," was the reply, "it does, but I propose to choose the color." And the color the Christian chooses is hope. "Why are you cast down, O my soul, and why are you disquieted within me? Hope in God; for I shall again praise Him, my help, and my God" (Psalm 42:11). Hope has to have a basis for expecting. Our hope is based on God Himself. "For we are saved by hope" (Romans 8:24).

A Realistic Hope

Summing up, we may say that Christian hope is confidence in God, the willingness to entrust to Him the tomorrows of our life. It is a *realistic* hope fully realizing that tomorrow may not be better than today. Tomorrow we may suffer. Tomorrow we may fall. Tomorrow we may die. But tomorrow, too, like today, God will be with us, sustaining us, upholding us, supporting us with His everlasting arms, bringing good out of evil, granting life in death.

False Hopes

Man has been putting his faith in a lot of false hopes; progress, scientific humanism, Communism, education, politics, the welfare state, etc. But all of these are secular substitutes for the Kingdom of God. They have let us down and have produced greater hopelessness than ever. Our hopefulness is based not on the schemes of men but on God. "We have set our hope on the living God, Who is the Savior of all men, especially of those who believe" (I Tim. 4:10).

A Gift to Share

Hope is indeed one of God's greatest gifts to us. But it is a gift that God expects us to share with others. St. Paul advised his friends in Thessalonica to give this precious gift to others, "Encourage one another and build one another up . . . Encourage the fainthearted . . . Rejoice always." Often the gift people need most and the one we withhold the most is hope. And yet it is not such a difficult thing to give. A moment's thoughtfulness, a pause to reflect on another's needs, and hope can be given at no greater cost than a friendly word or a warming smile. "The best thing a psychiatrist can do for his patients is to light them a candle of hope," said Dr. Karl Menninger. "Hope is the medicine I use more than any other," said a cardiologist. But one doesn't have to be a psychiatrist or a cardiologist to spread hope. Every Christian can share his hope in Christ with others.

So instead of cursing the darkness, light a candle of hope for others—not a false hope but a hope based on the greatest reality there is:

—the reality of God's forgiveness;
—the reality of God's strength for our everyday needs;
—the reality of His guidance for our confusion;

—the reality of Christ's victory over our death;
—the reality of God's infinite love in Christ for each one of us.

Recently an American visited Mother Teresa's "Home for the Dying" in Calcutta, India. When Mother Teresa saw people dying in the streets of Calcutta, she was so moved that on her own, she dragged their dying bodies into a deserted temple which she had cleaned up. There she provided loving care. "Every human being at least deserves to have somebody loving them while they are dying," she said.

When the visitor arrived at the home, the place was filled. There were narrow, low ceilings and dim lights, but everything smelled clean and sweet. One of the nurses told the visitor, "An interesting thing is happening. We accept only those who are dying of a terminal disease. But the amazing thing is that when they come here and feel the love of Christ, they are filled with hope and many of them stop dying. In fact, we're thinking of changing our name to "Home for the Living!"

"When many of them come here and feel the love of Christ, *they are filled with hope.*"

"We have set our hope in the living God, who is the Savior of all men, especially of those who believe" (I Tim. 4:10).

We close with St. Paul's great benediction to the Romans: "May the God of hope fill you with all joy and peace in believing, so that by the power of the Holy Spirit you may abound in hope" (Romans 15:13).

The Sacred Writings Which Instruct for Salvation

The Sixteenth Sunday of Luke (2 Timothy 3:10-15)

> *" . . . from childhood you have been acquainted with the sacred writings which are able to instruct you for salvation through faith in Christ Jesus" (2 Timothy 3:15).*

When Martin Heidegger, the German philosopher was asked some time ago whether he was an atheist he replied, "No, because I do not deny the existence of God; I merely say that He is absent." Heidegger's remark describes how many people feel today. They do not deny that God exists. But they live with little sense of His presence. God is absent from their experience, from their lives.

The sense of God's absence is not new. Thousands of years ago the prophet Amos spoke of God hiding Himself. He warned:

> "Behold, the days are coming, says the Lord God, when I will send a famine on the land; not a famine of bread, nor a thirst for water, but of hearing the words of the Lord. They shall wander from sea to sea, and from north to east; they shall run to and fro to seek the word of the Lord, but they shall not find it."

Job's famous struggle was basically a search for God who seemed reluctant to make a stage appearance for him. "O that

I knew where I might find Him! That I might come even to His seat," he cried.

Does God hide? St. John Chrysostom answered this question once. How can He Who is the Light of the World possibly hide? Yet, he said, even though the sun shines and is everywhere present it is the easiest thing in the world for man to shut out the rays of the sun and create darkness. All he has to do is to close his eyelids and he is in complete darkness.

God is not absent. Rather it is man who does not want God around. It is man who is absent from God. There are several reasons for this. One is *apathy*. People have no time for God. They are too busy with other things. God is absent because there is little desire on the part of people to have Him present. Time and time again the Bible insists that only those who seek God find God. He doesn't come where He is not wanted. He forces no one.

But God's absence does not mean that God is not interested. He may be absent because man does not want Him around, but He is forever waiting to be found. There is an old story about a boy who was playing hide-and-seek with his friends. He was thrilled when it came his turn to hide. But while he was hiding, the other boys lost interest and went off. The boy was heart-broken. His grandfather found him sobbing and said, "Don't weep because your friends didn't come to find you. Perhaps you can learn from this disappointment that God too is waiting to be found and men have gone off in search of other things."

If God is absent from many people today, it is because of our apathy, our pride, our moral indifference. But God is still waiting—in the quietness, in the shadow—waiting to be found.

Scribbled on the wall of a cellar in Cologne, Germany, during the violence and despair of World War II was this profound confession of faith:

"I believe in the sun, even when it is not shining;

I believe in love, even when I feel it not;
I believe in God, even when He is silent."

God is not silent unless we want Him to be. Of old He spoke through the prophets. In these last days He has spoken supremely in the person of His Son Jesus Christ. He continues to speak to each of us today.

How?

If Only I Could Hear Him!

There are people who say, "If I had the opportunity to hear God speak in person, I would run on my bare feet to the ends of the earth to hear Him." But God is present here and now and He is speaking to each of us personally. We do not have to travel to the ends of the earth to hear Him. He speaks to us all the time in and through His Word, the Holy Bible. What is the Bible but the Word of God speaking to us in church, at home, wherever we may be. It is God's Word just as surely as if God Himself were speaking to us.

". . . from childhood you have been acquainted with the sacred writings which are able to instruct you for salvation through faith in Christ Jesus" (2 Tim. 3:15).

St. Chrysostom writes, "As when God became man in Bethlehem the eternal Word became flesh, so in the Bible the glory of God veils itself in the fleshly garment of human thought and human language." God is speaking!

Whenever we pick up the Bible to read, we need to say to ourselves, "God is now speaking to me." He speaks not in thunder in lightning as He spoke to Moses on Mt. Sinai. He speaks to us as Jesus spoke to His disciples in the Sermon on the Mount. He sat down with them on a lovely meadow and spoke to them personally the words of life.

As Dr. Pius Parsch writes, "The Bible is the living, actual word of God—to me and to you. When you are reading the Bible, you are not just reading something which God spoke (to others) in the dim and distant past. God is speaking to you *now*. Bible reading is a conversation with God; we are actually in contact with Him, and how greatly we ought to prize that fact! When you say your prayers you are *speaking* to God; when you read the Bible God *is speaking to you*—not as a stern judge but as a loving Father."

God speaks! Do we listen? Do we read? Every day every daily newspaper in the country has a horoscope. Millions look to astrology through the horoscope for daily guidance. Avidly, they study the position of the stars seeking to find in them the answers to their problems. All along, the Word of God is present in every home, in every hotel room. Yet, if it remains a closed book, is it a wonder that for many people today God is so absent that they turn to the stars for guidance?

God doesn't have to be absent. In fact, He doesn't want to be absent—not He Who took the name EMMANUEL: *God with us*. Do you remember what it was that helped American P.O.W.'s survive those terrible years in North Vietnamese prisons? It was the Bible. They exchanged Scripture verses—secretly whispering them to one another, writing them on toilet paper, and tapping them out in Morse code. The Bible filled them with the assurance of God's presence, and they were able to survive a confinement that otherwise might have destroyed them mentally, physically, and spiritually.

When under brutal mental torture, they found that the only way that could prevent a breakdown was by feeding their minds on God's promises which they had hidden in their minds and hearts.

Dostoevsky

The great Russian Orthodox writer Dostoevsky, spent four years in a prison camp in Siberia. While there, he went through what he called "unspeakable, interminable suffering." The only thing that provided the comfort and strength he needed to survive was a small New Testament two Christian women had given him on his way to Siberia. It remained with him all his life and was read to his children on his deathbed.

Informs, Reforms, Transforms

"Most books *in*form, a few *re*form, the Bible alone *trans*forms" someone said. The truth is that the Bible does *all three.* It *in*forms us about Jesus the Son of God Whom to know is eternal life. It *re*forms us for in it we find the ideal and the standard by which we ought to live. It *trans*forms us because in it we are brought face to face with the grace and power of Christ by which all things are made new. Information, reformation, transformation—the Bible has all of them.

He Steps Out of the Bible

"Jesus Christ seemed to come right out of the Bible," said one of the teenagers from downtown New York who had been a drug addict. He had been saved through the magnificent ministry of the Rev. David Wilkerson. "He (Jesus) became a living person who wanted to stand with me through my problems." The power of God for salvation—that is what the Gospel is. God's power steps out of the Bible right into your life and mine!

"It Finds Me"

One of the finest tributes ever paid to the Bible was that of Coleridge, the poet. He said simply, "It finds me." This is another aspect of the power of the Gospel for salvation: "It finds me." It finds me in my wrong doing and convicts me of sin. It finds me in my loneliness and brings to me the companionship of God. It finds me in my need and brings the divine answer to the need. Are we giving the word of God a chance to find us?

A Love Letter

A young boy, eager to communicate with just anyone outside the walls of his orphanage, wrote the following words on a slip of paper: "To anyone who finds this, I love you." The wind blew the paper out beyond the walls to the world. In like manner, the Bible is God's love note to you and me. Its message is: "To anyone who reads this. I love you" Signed: "J.C."

The Bible is more than a love letter, it is a love letter that contains a proposal for marriage from God to you. He wishes to enter into the most intimate possible relationship of love with you. He delivers the proposal to you through the Bible. He expects a response. It is the most important response you will ever make. Will you say "Yes" or "No" to your Creator, your Savior, your God? Your eternal destiny depends on your response.

When Elizabeth Barrett became the wife of Robert Browning, her parents disowned her because they disapproved of the marriage. The daughter, however, wrote almost every week, telling them that she loved them and longed for a reconciliation. After 10 years she received a huge box in the mail that contained all the notes she had sent. Not one had been opened! Although these "love letters" have become an invaluable part of classical English literature, it's really pathetic to think that they were never read by Elizabeth Barrett's parents. Had they looked at just one, the broken relationship with their daughter might have been healed.

The Bible is the box containing all of God's love letters to us. They express His earnest longing for reconciliation, fellowship and union with us. They were *not* written to remain unopened. So take, read and discover God!

" . . . from childhood you have been acquainted with the sacred writings which are able to instruct you for salvation through faith in Christ Jesus" (2 Tim. 3:15).

The Body Is Meant for the Lord

The Seventeenth Sunday of Luke (I Corinthians 6:12-20)

"The body is not meant for immorality, but for the Lord, and the Lord for the body" (I Cor. 6:13).

There is increaseing interest in the body today. Jogging, calisthenics, tennis, swimming, lifting weights: Americans are huffing and puffing as never before to get into better shape. Sports and health clubs are constantly advertising the merits of regular exercise. Great emphasis is placed on proper diet, health foods, sufficient vitamins and weight watching. Billions of dollars and hours are spent in trying to keep the body healthy.

Yet at the same time seldom before have we been doing more to degrade the body. I cannot remember when there was more pornography being served than today: in "adult" stores, movies, television, best sellers and magazines, the human body is being terribly degraded. Statistics on VD are the highest they have ever been. The use of alcohol, cigarettes and drugs is at its highest. The same people who join health clubs and go on crash diets are dissipating themselves in other ways, degrading the very body they are trying to preserve.

Thus, while on the one hand, the body is being exalted; on the other hand, it is being exploited, manipulated, and played with. It is not being respected and used properly.

Part of the reason for this is that we have lost sight of God

Who created the body. We need, in other words, a theology of the body. And this is what St. Paul gives us in today's Epistle lesson. He restores our vision of God and what He means to the human body. He tells us that the gospel of Jesus is a gospel that relates to our bodies.

The Body Is for the Lord

First, Paul tells us that "the body is not meant for immorality but for the Lord." The body was created for God, not for immorality. In baptism, the sign of the cross was made on each member of the body, thus dedicating each member to the service of Christ. Paul says in Romans 12, "I appeal to you, therefore, brethren, by the mercies of God, to present your bodies as a living sacrifice, holy and acceptable to God, which is your spiritual worship." We are to worship and serve God not only with our mind and heart but with the total person which includes the body. The body is for the Lord. It even functions best when it is used to serve Him. It begins to break down when it is used to serve immorality, unchastity, lust, and self-indulgence.

The Lord Is for the Body

Paul tells us not only that the body is for the Lord but also that the Lord is for the body. This means that the great salvation Jesus died to make possible affects the body. Jesus died and rose again not just for the soul but also for the body. The body is sacred. It is a temple of the living God. "Do you not know that your body is a temple of the Holy Spirit within you, which you have from God?" (I Cor. 6:19). God will not leave this body to rot in a grave. He will raise it up to dwell with Him forever. "And God raised the Lord and will also raise us up by His power" (I Cor. 6:14). It is not just the soul that will spend eternity with God. This very body in which we now live will be raised to spend eternity with God. This very body in which we now live will be raised to spend eternity with its

Lord and Master. As St. Paul says in Romans 8:11, "If the Spirit of him who raised Jesus from the dead dwells in you, he who raised Jesus from the dead will give life to your mortal bodies also through his Spirit which dwells in you."

God Will Raise and Transform the Body

Although this temple in which we live may be put in a grave, one day it will be raised and transformed into the likeness of the Lord Jesus Christ. The body is not finished when it is put into a coffin; it is destined to be brought into the very presence of God. The body is for the Lord and the Lord for the body.

Our body is God's. We cannot play fast and loose with it, because it is for His use. Not only is it going to be transformed into His likeness, but we shall be held responsible before the judgment seat of Christ for the deeds done in the body.

Your Bodies Are Members of Christ

"Do you not know that your bodies are members of Christ?" asks Paul in today's Epistle lesson. "Shall I therefore take the members of Christ and make them members of a prostitute? Never! Do you not know that He who joins himself to a prostitute becomes one body with her? For, as it is written, 'The two shall become one.' But he who is united to the Lord becomes one spirit with him. Shun immorality. Every other sin which a man commits is outside the body; but the immoral man sins against his own body" (I Cor. 6:15-18).

Shall the Christian take that which is a member of Christ and give it to some unworthy use? Shall he take his body, this temple of the living God, and yield it, surrender it, to the immoral, sinful purposes of Satan? What will happen if he does? He becomes one body with that which is sinful if he joins himself to it. But as a Christian he is already joined to Christ, being "one Spirit with Him." Shall he destroy this union with Christ to establish a union with Satan?

You Are Not Your Own

But cannot man do what he likes with his own body? Isn't this what is meant when they tell us that anything goes between two "consenting adults"? That is exactly what Paul denies in today's Epistle lesson. He calls it a lie. That can't possibly be true for Christians, he says. Your body is not your own. It belongs to God, just as much as your soul. It has been redeemed by Christ, just as much as your soul. A price has been paid for your body—an expensive price, the very blood of Jesus. Far from belonging to you, the body is God's temple and must be kept holy for Him. "Haven't you yet learned that your body is the home of the Holy Spirit God gave you, and that He lives within you? Your own body does not belong to you. For God has bought you with a great price. So use every part of your body to give glory back to God, because He owns it" (I Cor. 6:19-20).

PRAYER

Now unto Him Who loved us and gave Himself for us, making us members of His Body and temples of the Holy Spirit: to Him be all glroy, honor, worship, praise and thanksgiving now and ever and unto ages of ages. Amen.

By Faith They Conquered Kingdoms

The Sunday Before the Birth of Christ (Hebrews 11:9-10, 32-40)

"And what more shall I say? For time would fail me to tell of Gideon, Barak, Samson, Jeptha, of David and Samuel and the prophets—who through faith conquered kingdoms, enforced justice, received promises, stopped the mouths of lions, quenched raging fire, escaped the edge of the sword, won strength out of weakness, became mighty in war, put foreign armies to flight" (Hebrews 11:32-34).

Since the Epistle lesson today speaks of the great accomplishments of faith, it is appropriate that I share with you one clergyman's definition of faith. He was comparing the difference between fact and faith in his sermon. "That you are sitting before me in this church," he said, "is a fact. That I am standing, speaking from this pulpit is a fact. But it is only faith that makes me believe anyone is listening to me."

Another pastor looked at his congregation one Sunday and said, "I see you are back to have your faith lifted."

The Epistle lesson tells of the great accomplishments wrought by faith in the lives of Abraham, Barak, Samson Jephtha, David, Samuel and the prophets—who "through faith conquered kingdoms . . . received promises . . . won strength out of weakness, became mighty in war, put foreign armies to flight" (Hebrews 11:32-34).

Amazing Faith

How amazing this thing called faith. For example, how amazing that the shepherds, when the heavens were opened and the angels sang, could have believed that a Savior was born in Bethlehem and would be found in a cave among animals. How amazing! How unbelievable! They should have said, "How can this be? Why should God open the heavens so that angels should sing to lowly shepherds? Surely, if God had an announcement to make, He would make it to Herod or to the high priest, not to us." How astonishing that the shepherds should have believed that they would find God's Son being born not in a palace but in a stable! *Yet* they believed!

How amazing that the Wise Men believed when they came to Jerusalem and found no festivities for the birth of a prince. All was still. There would have been more commotion if a calf or lamb had been born. The Wise Men might well have gone home. Instead, they inquired and searched the Scriptures, and did not hesitate to go to tiny Bethlehem. How amazing that they should believe that the Prince of Peace, the Wonderful Counselor, the Savior of the world, the Promised Messiah, would be born in a backwoods village instead of at Rome or Athens! Yet they believed!

What Faith Is Not

What is this thing called faith?

Let us begin with a few examples of what faith is *not*. Faith is not a storm cellar to which we flee for refuge from the storms of life. It is, instead, an inner force which gives us the strength to face those storms and their consequences with serenity of spirit. In times of greatest stress, faith has the miraculous power to lift to greatness ordinary persons like

"Gideon, Barak, Samson, Jephtha, David and Samuel."

Faith is not trust in yourself which is doomed to disappointment. It is not trust in your friends who will one day die and leave you. It is not trust in money which will one day be taken away from you. It is not trust in reputation which some slanderous tongue can so easily blast. Faith is trust in God Who will never leave you or forsake you in time or in eternity.

Faith is not speculation. When someone asked Michael Faraday, "What are your speculations?" he replied, "Speculations? I have none! I am resting on certainties. 'I know whom I have believed and am persuaded that he is able to keep that which I have committed unto him against that day' " (2 Tim. 1:12).

Faith is not looking at the waves; it is looking instead at the Lord Who walks upon the waves. If I keep my eyes on that Lord, the water and the spray will still be there, but they cannot do a thing to me any more. For I have placed my life in the very hands of Him Whom the wind and the waves obey. Faith is resting all my weight in those hands.

What Faith Is

What else is faith? Here are some short but very meaningful definitions:

Faith doesn't know where it is being led, but it knows Who is leading.

Faith in Christ does for us what sunshine does for stained-glass windows.

Faith is charting your tomorrows not by the stars (your horoscope) but by the One Who made the stars.

Faith is man's response to the promises and possibilities of God.

Faith is looking at a new born baby, and seeing the Creator.

Faith is walking in the rain and knowing the sun will shine again.

Faith is facing crucifixion, and knowing that it is not the final chapter of life. "In the world you have tribulation, but be of good cheer, I have overcome the world," said Jesus.

Faith has a Siamese twin named love. In fact, if love is not attached to faith, it is dead. Faith receives, love gives.

Faith is nurtured; it grows by prayer and the study of God's word. "Faith comes from what is heard, and what is heard comes by the preaching of Christ" (Romans 10:17).

St. John writes, "This is the victory that overcomes the world, our faith. Who is it that overcomes the world but he who believes that Jesus is the Son of God?" (I John 5:4-5).

Faith is taking God at His word just as you believe the scientist when he tells you that the sun is 92 million miles away from the earth even though you have never measured it.

Faith is bowing down to what God reveals. "If we receive the testimony of man, the testimony of God is greater; for this is the testimony of God that he has borne witness to His Son . . . He who does not believe God has made Him a liar, because he has not believed in the testimony that God has borne to His Son" (I John 5:9-11).

Faith is to say with strong conviction, and mean it, I believe—I believe that I shall see the goodness of the Lord in the land of the living. I believe that the Lord is my light and my salvation; whom shall I fear? I believe that the Lord is the stronghold of my life; of whom shall I be afraid?" (Psalm 27).

Faith does not go against reason; it goes beyond reason.

Faith is betting one's life that Jesus is the Son of God and the Savior of the world and risking everything for it. "By faith, Samson, Barak. . . . " and the sentence goes on to describe the splendid risks their faith took for God.

Faith is not just to believe in the existence of God but to put yourself in His hands; to know not only that God is but that He cares.

Faith is the hand that takes the blessing.

Faith receives what God gives, not as something we deserve, but as a gift of His grace.

Faith Holds Fast to Christ

The story is told of two men who fell into a river above a roaring cataract. One man seized a rope thrown in his direction by people on shore. The other hung for dear life to a heavy log which came floating by. Both men were clinging to something, but only the man who held fast to the rope was saved.

Faith holds fast to Christ, the Savior of the world. It latches on to Him, because there is salvation in no other.

Faith is the marriage of Christ—the Bridegroom—to the bride which is my soul.

Faith is the handle by which I grasp God's power and apply it to my weakness.

Faith is remembering when I feel utterly worthless that I am the one for whom God gave His Son.

Faith is the assurance that God is working out a plan for good in my life even though things seem to be going against me.

Faith is believing that God still loves me and is working for my supreme good even when He says "no" to my prayers.

Faith is not worrying about what the future holds because we know and trust the One Who holds the future.

Faith is the astronaut who says, "We're in trouble out here in this capsule in outer space but I have faith in those guys in ground control back in Houston."

Faith is reason at rest in God (St. Augustine).

The opposite of faith is not unbelief but pessimism.

Faith is not throwing away the ticket and jumping off the train when it enters a dark tunnel. It is trusting the engineer to lead us through the darkness to light.

Faith is like a chalice. Each of us brings a chalice of faith to the altar, and each is filled according to its size. "According to your faith be it done to you," said Jesus (Matthew 9:30). How big is your chalice?

Faith is the eye by which we look to Jesus; the hand by

which we lay hold of Jesus; the tongue by which we taste how good the Lord is; the foot by which we go to Jesus.

Faith is *F*orsaking *A*ll *I* *T*ake *H*im.

Faith is man's hand reaching up to grasp the outstretched hand of God's grace. "By grace you are saved through faith" (Eph. 2:8).

Faith is a leap, a jump, a plunge not into a black void but into the arms of Someone Who loved me and gave Himself for me.

Faith looks forward "to the city which has foundations, whose builder and maker is God" (Heb. 11:10).

Faith is what enabled Gideon, Barak, Samson, Jephtha, David, Samuel, the prophets, and millions of others to endure fire, danger, sword; to conquer kingdoms; to win strength out of weakness.

Faith Makes a Difference

If you believe that there is no one at the helm of this universe, that you are just whirling through space endlessly, then you have a right to be angry and mad, to go crazy and end it all. But if you have faith and believe that there is Someone in charge of this universe; that that Someone is the God who "so loved the world that He gave His only Son so that whoever believes in Him might not perish but have life everlasting," then you, too, like Gideon and countless others, can conquer kingdoms.

Canst thou take the barren soil
And with all thy pains and toil
    make lilies grow?
Thou canst not, O helpless man,
Have faith in God. He can!

Canst thou paint the clouds at eve,
And all the sunset colors weave into
    the sky?

Thou canst not, O powerless man,
Have faith in God. He can!

Canst thou still thy troubled heart
And make cares and doubts depart
  from out thy soul?
Thou canst not, O faithless man,
Have faith in God. He can!

When the Time Had Fully Come

Christmas Day (Galatians 4:4-7)

"But when the time had fully come, God sent forth His Son, born of woman, born under the law, to redeem those who were under the law, so that we might receive adoption as sons". (Gal. 4:4-5).

The noted theologian Emil Brunner compares the coming of Jesus to the coming of a surgeon to perform life-giving surgery on a patient. God looks down on the world, he says, just as a doctor sits at the bed of a sick person delirious with fever who is not even aware of the doctor's presence. The doctor listens carefully to his breathing and takes his pulse. Then at a particular moment he calls the nurse and says, "Now is the time. Get him ready for surgery immediately."

Like a doctor, God stood by the side of suffering humanity for centuries listening carefully to man's spiritual breathing and taking the pulse of his soul. Suddenly, "when the time had fully come," He decided that the time had come for surgery. It was to be such delicate surgery that the Master Surgeon decided to come down from heaven to perform the surgery Himself.

Not By Chance

God set the time for the sending of His Son into the world. Christmas did not happen by chance. Christ's birth was no climactic evolutionary event. Rather it was God invading history at His right time. God took long years to get ready for it, and it happened when He wanted it to happen. When God's hour struck, Christ was born. That was "when the time had fully come," the right time, God's time.

God is intelligent enough to have a plan and a purpose for the people He created.

A Prepared World

There was nothing accidental or by chance in the coming of Christ. He came in the fulness of time at the end of a period of preparation.

He came at the end of a long period of *prophetic* preparation. As Peter said to the Roman Centurion, "To Him (Christ) all the prophets bear witness." When the Wise Men asked Herod where the King of the Jews was born, Herod consulted his own wise men and without any hesitation they told him "in Bethlehem of Judea." His coming had ben foretold by the prophets.

The world was prepared not only *prophetically* but also *politically*. The Roman Empire had unified the world. Everywhere barriers were down. The world was one big neighborhood. Roads were not blocked by national frontiers. The seas were not closed by pirates. Roman peace prevailed. There was freedom of travel in the great Roman Empire. If Christ had come earlier, Christianity could have been strangled in its cradle because of the strife and wars among nations.

Now the missionaries could walk freely over roads and bridges built by Rome to carry the gospel to the ends of the earth. Now they could speak the one language that was spoken and understood everywhere throughout the Roman Empire: Greek. It was a language just waiting to be used by the Apostles in their preaching, teaching, and writing.

The time had fully come not only prophetically,

politically, linguistically but also *morally* and *religiously*. The old gods of Greece and Rome were either dead or dying. Pagan Greece with all of its wisdom and great philosophers would go for guidance to a drugged and hallucinating peasant girl at the oracle of Delphi. The world was at a low ebb morally when Christ came.

It was a world that was waiting for a Savior. A world where almost every other person was a slave; a world that was ready for the doctrine that "there is neither male nor female, Jew or Gentile, slave or free but in Christ all are one," all free, all equal. A world that was seething in immorality was ready for the message of Jesus, "Blessed are the pure in heart for they shall see God." A world that was lost in darkness was ready for Him Who was and is the Light of the World. A world that was writhing in the despair of death was ready for Him Who is "the Resurrection and the life." The world was waiting in agony for the One Who would bring hope, peace, justice, love, equality.

God Sent Forth His Son

When the time had fully come—and it had come prophetically, politically, linguistically, morally, and religiously—*God sent forth His Son*. Not prophets any more. Not patriarchs any more. Not priests. Not angels from heaven. Not kings. But His own Son.

"In many and various ways God spoke of old to our fathers by the prophets; but in these last days he has spoken to us by a Son, whom he appointed the heir of all things, through whom also he created the world" (Hebrews 1:1-2).

"The true light that enlightens every man was coming into the world. He was in the world, and the world was made through him, yet the world knew him not . . . And the word became flesh and dwelt among us, full of grace and truth; we have beheld his glory, glory as of the only Son from the Father . . . And from his fulness have we all received, grace upon grace. For the law was given through Moses; grace and truth came through Jesus Christ" (John 1:9-10; 14; 16-17).

God cared enough to send His very best. He spared not His own Son. "But last of all he sent unto them his Son, saying, 'They will reverence my Son.' "

"To Redeem Them"

"When the time had fully come, God sent forth his Son . . . " Why? For what purpose? Surely, all that long and careful preparation through the centuries must have had a tremendously great purpose. Such a great sacrifice on the part of God the Father must have had an exalted purpose. St. Paul reveals the purpose: "to redeem those who were under the law." To redeem sinners under the sentence of death. That was the way Paul put it. "To all who received him . . . he gave power to become children of God" (John 1:11). That was the way the Apostle John put it. Redeemed with the precious blood of Christ, made "partakers of the divine nature" (2 Peter 1:4). That was the way Peter put it. And Jesus put it this way: "The Son of Man came to seek and to save that which was lost."

St. Gregory of Nyssa put it this way:

"Do you ask why God was born among man?"

"Here is the reason for God's presence among man. Our nature was sick and needed a doctor. Man had fallen and needed someone to raise him up. He Who had ceased to participate in the good needed someone to bring him back to it. He who was shut up in darkness needed the presence of life. The prisoner was looking for someone to ransom him, the captive for someone to take his part. He who was under the yoke of slavery was looking for someone to set him free. Were these trifling and unworthy reasons to impel God to come down and visit human nature . . . ?"

"Adoption as Sons"

Here then is the grand purpose of His coming: "to redeem those who were under the law *that we might receive adoption as sons.*" He did all that that we might get back that place in the family of God which we had lost through sin. "See what love the Father has given us, that we should be called children of God, and so we are" (I John 3:1). "No longer do I call you servants, for the servant does not know what his master is doing; but I have called you friends, for all that I have heard from my Father I have made known to you" (John 15:15).

"*Adoption as sons.*" It is more of an honor to be an adopted child than a naturally-born child. A natural child in a family might *not* be there by choice of the parents. It may have come into the world unwanted, a biological accident. It may be excess baggage, just another mouth to feed. Not so the adopted child who is wanted, sought for, and chosen. We are God's adopted children.

When parents adopt children, they look for the best child available. They check the child's parents, background, intelligence, and personality. But God's grace, in adopting us as His children, stooped down to accept us while we were yet sinners, disobedient, and rebellious.

In the process of adoption, it is God's grace again that takes the initiative to adopt us. We do not adopt Him as our Father. He adopts us as His children in the Sacrament of Baptism before we ever know Him or love Him or choose Him. "You did not choose me," said Jesus, "but I have chosen you" (John 15:16).

"If a Son Then an Heir"

If we are sons of God, then we are heirs (Gal. 4:7). "So through God you are no longer a slave but a son, and if a son then an heir" (Gal. 4:7). There are poor people who seek to marry rich people so that they may become through marriage heirs of great fortunes. But here the tables are turned. God's love chooses to marry itself to us that we might become His heirs. Jesus came as the Bridegroom seeking to establish a marriage relationship with each one of us. Ours is the privilege of choosing to become His bride.

"If a son then an heir." The coming of Christ is the regaining of our inheritance. We are no longer disinherited or disowned. We are not only sons but heirs. And our inheritance is not all beyond the river we call death. This is where some of us make a great mistake. We are not only heirs of great expectations beyond, but of great possessions here and now.

As heirs we inherit the riches of God's grace. We inherit God's love. We inherit the joy of salvation. We inherit peace of mind as a gift from God. We share in His great triumph and victory over death. We have the mercy of God in terms of forgiveness. Eternity is ours. Heaven is ours. These blessings are ours not because we deserve them. They come to us because by His grace we have become sons and heirs of the Father. It is through this inheritance that we become unbelievably rich. "Though He was rich, yet for our sakes He became poor so that by His poverty we might become rich," said Paul.

"What Did You Get for Christmas?"

How often we hear after Christmas the question, "What did you get for Christmas?" It is a good question but the emphasis is on getting. A better question would be, "What did you give for Christmas?"—especially to the poor, the starving, the deprived. An even better question would be, "What did you get *from* Christmas?" Did you accept God's great gift of His Son? Have you said "yes" to His proposal for marriage? Have you repented to accept His redemption from sin? Have you really become His son or daughter? And if a son or daughter, then an heir? Have you claimed your inheritance in Christ?

PRAYER

Lord, You sent forth Your Son . . . to redeem *me*, that *I* might receive the adoption of sons . . . that through Your grace I might no longer be a slave but a son, and if a son then an heir. But this does not happen automatically, Lord. I must choose. I must believe. I must obey. I must follow. I do so now, Lord, on this day of Your Birth. I yield my life to You completely. Redeem me. Reclaim me. Make me Your son or daughter, Your heir. Amen.

Does Life Have a Plot?

The Sunday Before Theophany (2 Timothy 4:5-8)

"I have fought the good fight, I have finished the race, I have kept the faith. Henceforth there is laid up for me the crown of righteousness, which the Lord, the righteous judge, will award to me on that day, and not only to me but also to all who have loved his appearance." (2 Timothy 4:7-8)

For many people today the trouble with life is that it has no plot. The Rockefeller Report on Education in 1958 included these significant words:

"What most people, young or old, want is not merely security or comfort or luxury—although they are glad to have these. They want meaning in their lives. If their era and their culture and their leaders do not or cannot offer them great meanings, great objectives, great convictions, then they will settle for shallow and trivial meanings."

Why Drugs?

A leading psychiatrist said recently on the subject of drug abuse:

"Let me now explain my general gloom. We tend to think that drug abuse is a disease for which we can find a cure. We speak loosely of a vaccine against the heroin epidemic, overlooking the fact that drug abuse is what people inflict on themselves. They inflict it on themselves because they cannot find meaning in a lost and joyless society."

Someone said once, "Life must go on. I forget just why." That's our problem: no plot, no meaning, no purpose, no goal, no mission.

Why Abortions?

Why do many people today adopt such a brutal attitude toward unborn human life? Is it not due to the fact that they have a very dim view of human life in any form? People know neither who they are nor where they are going. They feel that life is senseless, irrational, without point or meaning. Many do not really know why they should not commit suicide. And since this is the case, what difference does it make whether one sucks a human fetus (an unborn human baby) into an early death with a vacuum instrument before birth or the poor creature dies 40 or 70 years later? We have such a low view of the unborn because we have such a low view of the born, the living.

The High View of Life

Contrast this low view of life with the high view expressed by St. Paul in today's epistle lesson:

"I have fought the good fight, I have finished the race, I have kept the faith. Henceforth there is laid up for me the crown of righteousness, which the Lord, the righteous judge, will award to me on that Day, and not only to me but also to all who have loved his appearing."

The place to find great purpose for our lives is still at the feet of Jesus—where St. Paul found it. Here life's true meaning can be realized. After an encounter with Christ, we know that life has a plot. It leads somewhere. It has a mission. It can result in the peace that passes all understanding.

The Low View of Life

Life is viewed as being empty and meaningless by many

great thinkers who do not believe in God. Here are a few quotations from people with brilliant minds, but who have not been illuminated by the truth of God:

"Life is a pilgrimage from nowhere to nowhere."

"Man is a sick fly, taking a dizzy ride on a gigantic wheel."

"Life is but a hollow bubble."

"The time man spends here has no more meaning than that of the humblest insect, crawling from one annihilation to another."

Macbeth, as the shadows close about him in Shakespeare's play, says:

"Life's but a walking shadow, a poor player,
That struts and frets his hour upon the stage,
And then is heard no more; it is a tale
Told by an idiot, full of sound and fury,
Signifying nothing."

Life to Macbeth was a drama of unrelated moments with no sense and no plot.

In contrast to such hopelessness, how refreshing are the inspired words of Paul: "I have fought the good fight. . . . Now there is laid up for me the crown of righteousness."

Life Is Christ

The following bit of verse was written by an anonymous poet: "What is life?" asked a little child / As he romped on a golden day / Out of his life the answer came: 'Life is play! Life is play!' / 'What is life?' asked the sturdy man / As he toiled through the sun and rain, / And the woe in his heart cried out aloud, / 'Life is pain.' 'Life is pain' / "What is life?' asked the old, old man / As he gazed on the stars above, / And his wise, wise heart sang joyfully, 'Life is Christ! Life is love!' "

To exist is the portion of every person, but life in all its fulness belongs only to those who have been united to Christ. "I came that they may have life, and have it abundantly" (John 10:10) said Jesus. "And this is eternal life, that they may know thee the only true God, and Jesus Christ whom thou hast sent" (John 17:3). Without Christ life is a hopeless end; with Christ it is endless hope.

Metropolitan Anthony Bloom, the great spiritual leader of the Russian Orthodox Church, was born into the home of a Russian ambassador. He grew up in Switzerland and Persia and later became a medical doctor in France. During World War II he was involved in the French resistance to the Nazis. During that period God called him to enter the priesthood.

The Metropolitan was asked once about the intense personal nature of his experience with God: "In Marxist terms, in the terms of any unbeliever, I am just a mental case," he said. "I was told that more than once, and I am quite prepared to be considered as such. My only problem is that, mad as I am, I have meaning in life . . . I have a joy that nothing has ever taken away from me, and people who are sane come to me to see how one can go mad!"

God's Sanity

What the Godless world calls insanity is the only kind of sanity. It is a sanity that gives meaning and joy to life.

Francois Mauriac, the French philosopher said:

> "I believe as I did as a child, that life has meaning, a direction, a value; that no suffering is lost, that every tear counts, and each drop of blood; and the secret of living in today's troubled world is found in the simple phrase of St. John, 'God is love.' "

God does not build roads that lead nowhere. All of God's roads lead somwhere:

"I consider that the sufferings of this present time are not worth comparing with the glory that is to be revealed to us" (Romans 8:18).

"Beloved, we are God's children now; it does not yet appear what we shall be, but we know that when He appears we shall be like Him, for we shall see Him as He is" (I John 3:2).

A young woman said to her psychiatrist, "Doctor, I need

something to look forward to." Christ always gives us something to look forward to. Despair comes not because the going gets hard, but because we doubt that the going means anything. With Christ the going had meaning for St. Paul: "I have finished the race. . . . Now there is laid up for me the crown of righteousness."

If Jesus is for real, everything fits. Everything has meaning. Without Him, nothing fits; nothing has meaning.

Last Tuesday evening in our young people's meeting we discussed the question: What is your mission in life? If someone gave you a pencil and paper and said, "Write down your mission in life," how would you answer?

I know how St. Paul would have answered: "For me to live is Christ" (Phil. 1:21). Because loving and serving Christ was his all-consuming mission in life, his life had such great meaning that he looked forward expectantly to the crown of righteousness which he would receive from his Master.

"I have kept the faith . . . Henceforth there is laid up for me the crown of righteousness."

PRAYER

Dear Lord, it is when I say "Yes" to You that life finds its great meaning. If I haven't said it before, let me say it now: Yes, Lord, I love You. Grant me the grace to follow You in all that I do. Amen.

Mature Manhood in Christ

The Sunday Following Theophany. Ephesians 4:7-13

"Until we all attain to . . . mature manhood, to the measure of the stature of the fulness of Christ" (Ephesians 4:13).

A novel of a few years ago, "Second Growth," dealt with life in a small town in Vermont, where there was very little opportunity for young people. A good teacher who was interested in a boy of fine promise, said to him, "I'd take this chance to go to college, if I were you. There won't be much else I could teach you around here. *You would stay the same size all your life.*"

"You would stay the same size all your life." An arresting sentence! It applies to many realms of life, besides that of a little town. We know that is just what happens to many people. They stay "the same size all their lives." Contrast this with the words of St. Paul in today's epistle lesson: "And his gifts were that some should be apostles, some prophets, some evangelists . . . for building up the body of Christ. Until we all attain . . . to mature manhood, to the measure of the stature of the fulness of Christ." (Ephesians 4:13). In our Christian life we are not to remain the same size. We are to grow "to mature manhood" becoming like Christ. As one quip put it: "Our pressing need today is for less publicity on how to stay young and more on how to grow up."

Immature Adults

A person thought about himself one day and said, "I have come to the conclusion that the greatest undeveloped territory in the world today lies under my hat." Room for growth!

Sometimes when we look at married people snarling and snapping at each other, when we see the way some so-called "adults" act, we would like to say, "Let's all grow up!"

We say this sort of thing to our children and at times rightfully so. Children ought to grow up. But to say this only to children is not enough. We need to say it to ourselves. How many miserable people there are—inflicting their miseries on one another and on their own children, because of their immaturity. They haven't grown up. And they don't want to grow up.

You are only young once, but you can stay immature indefinitely.

There are thousands of people who have never become adults, even though they may have celebrated their 18th or 21st birthday. Maturity, unfortunately, is not related to birthdays. Some people never become adults even at age 50. A great many of our problems today in the home, in marriage, in industry, are due to immaturity. We do not grow up. We remain the same size all our life.

Immaturity stands out as the number one troublemaker in causing mental, emotional and social ills.

Mature in Christ

To be mature is not enough for us Christians. The word of God calls on us to be mature in Christ. What does maturity in Christ mean? Negatively it means: putting away childish things, childish traits, and childish qualities of mind. As St. Paul said in the 13th chapter of First Corinthians, "When I was a child, I spoke as a child, I understood as a child, I thought as a child: but when I became a man, I put away childish things."

There are many traits that are charming in a child but disastrous in an adult.

One trait of a child, essential to his survival in the earliest days, is *self-centeredness*. It is a sort of mental blindness to the rest of the world. He doesn't see or care for other people. All he thinks of is himself.

"Put Away Childish Things"

A childish trait is that of knowing only one time: *today*. There's no tomorrow as far as the child is concerned. He wants what he wants and he wants it now.

A childish trait which has brought gray hairs to parents is the insistence on *having one's own way*. People who are adult infants live in a perpetual nursery, where they want others to respond instantly to their infantile cries.

A childish trait is that of resorting to unreasonable flights of anger. It is not that one should not be angry, but that he is angry at the wrong time and under the wrong circumstances. He is angry because his little world is disturbed, his ego touched, his false pride ruffled.

Another childish trait is scapegoating, that is, blaming others instead of ourselves. Like the little child we say, "Who me? I didn't do it. Johnny did it." Rather than accept responsibility for our failure, we place it on someone else. Rather than admit our sin and confess it, we hide it even though the price we pay is to be plagued by feelings of guilt and unworthiness.

When St. Paul learned that divisions had sprung up in the Corinthian church causing dissension, envy and jealousy, he wrote them his first epistle in which he said that he could not address them as mature Christians. "You are babes in Christ," he said. "You haven't been developing into Christian maturity. Consequently I have fed you with milk, not solid food, because you are not ready for stronger food. While there exist among you envying, strife and divisions, are you not immature?"

The Perfect Man

To be mature in Christ, then, means in its negative aspect to put away childish things: self-centeredness, insistence on having one's own way, anger, blaming others, envy, jealousy. To be a mature Christian in its positive aspect means to become more and more like Christ. Merely growing up is not enough. We are to grow up into something that is perfectly mature, and that for us Christians, is Christ. "Be ye perfect as I am perfect," said Jesus. Lecomte du Nouy, the French physicist, once wrote, "The perfect man is not a myth: he has lived in Christ." To be mature is to grow more and more like unto that perfect man: Jesus. "That you may grow up in all things into Him who is the head, even Christ" (Eph. 4:15).

The person who is mature in Christ is not the person who goes through life expecting to receive love, like the child, but the person who gives love; who produces love by loving. The person who is mature in Christ is the person who understands, who forgives, who accepts responsibility for his failures, who disciplines himself, who is humble, realizing that there is much he does not know and can never know.

St. Paul singles out love as the most important ingredient of maturity when he writes to the Colossians: "Above all put on love, which binds everything together in perfect harmony." It is when we allow Christ to come and live in us that we can achieve this kind of Godly maturity. Only He can give us the power to incarnate His love and maturity in our lives.

The Greatest Power in the World

There is a phrase in the Talmud which says, "Every blade of grass has its own angel that bends over it and whispers, 'Grow! Grow!' " The greatest power in the world is the power to grow. Look at the tiny acorn! For man this means not just physical growth. It means to channel this power to grow so that we may grow as Jesus grew: "in wisdom and stature and in favor with God and man." It means to grow mentally, physically, spiritually, socially and emotionally. It means to grow by God's grace from the image of God, in which we have been created, into the likeness of God which is Jesus. Through baptism we were born into the life of God. Now that we are born, we must grow in that life. Such growth "to mature manhood, to the measure of the stature of the fulness of Christ," can occur after baptism only through a dynamic personal relationship with Christ whereby He lives in us and we in Him. The essence of maturity is Jesus Christ, the most mature Man Who ever lived.

Those Who Have Finished Growing

A person quit the U.S. Patent Office in 1838 because he felt it had no future. All the inventions that were to be made, he felt, had been made. This is the mentality of the person who has ceased to grow. It is like the lady who said to the golfing pro when he asked her if she was interested in learning how to play the game: "No, thank you. My friend here is. But not me. I learned golf last week." Or the high school student who sat next to a famous astronomer at a dinner. When she found out he was a professor of astronomy, the teenager, wide eyed, said, "An astronomer. Really? I finished astronomy last year!"

It reminds me of those who "finished" Christianity when they finished Sunday school. They are now trying to deal with man-sized problems with a midget-sized faith in Christ and His power. They mature in other departments of life. But their Christian faith remains frozen at the childish level. And this cuts them off from receiving tremendous power in life. Someone defined the way to Christian growth this way:

G Go to God in prayer daily.
R Read God's word daily.
O Obey God, moment by moment.
W Witness for Christ by your life and words. .

"Grow," says Paul in today's Epistle lesson. Grow "to

mature manhood, to the measure of the stature of the fulness of Christ." "Grow in the grace and knowledge of our Lord and Savior Jeus Christ" (2 Peter 3:18). "Grow up in every way to Christ, who is the head" (Eph. 4:12). The result of this growth is described in Second Corinthians 3:18, "And we all, with unveiled face, beholding the glory of the Lord, are being changed into His likeness from one degree of glory to another; for this comes from the Lord . . ."

PRAYER

Lord, You placed this tremendous power to grow not only in the acorn but also in me. May the Holy Spirit guide me that I may grow more and more like unto the Perfect Man, Jesus, growing as He did "in wisdom and stature and in favor with God and man." Amen.

Now Is the Time of Salvation

Sixteenth Sunday of Matthew (2 Corinthians 6:1-10)

"Behold, now is the acceptable time; behold now is the day of salvation" (2 Cor. 6:2).

Hoping to inspire his workers with promptness and energy, a San Francisco executive posted a number of signs reading "Do It Now" throughout his factory and offices. When he was asked some weeks later how his staff had reacted, he shook his head sadly, "I don't even like to talk about it," he said. "The cashier skipped with five thousand dollars; the head accountant eloped with the best secretary I ever had; three typists asked for a raise; the factory workers voted to go out on strike; and the office boy joined the Navy."

Do it now!

There is a beautiful poem entitled "Do It Now" that I share with you:

It seems we have so little time
To do the kindly things.
Before we realize the truth
We find that time has wings.

We plan to give a word of cheer
To one who needs a friend
We plan to see someone who's ill
Who may be near the end.

And there's a letter we should write
    To someone who is sad;
Our words may be just what they need
    To cheer and make them glad.

It's easy to procrastinate
    And leave such tasks undone;
But such a course will bring regrets
    When life's short race is run.

There is a cure for all these ills
    Just three words tell us how
To bring a speedy, perfect cure,
    They're simply: "Do it now!"
        —Author unknown

St. Paul writes in the epistle lesson today, "Behold, now is the accepted time; behold, now is the time of salvation." In other words, do it now.

The Happiest Period

A psychologist once asked 3,000 persons "What are you living for?" He was startled to find that most of them were simply enduring the present while they waited for something better in the future. Actors and entertainers doing small parts were waiting for the "big chance." People in business were thinking of their present jobs as drudgery, a mere marking of time, until fate opened the door to something better.

One middle-aged mother said, "I only hope that my nerves can stand the ordeal until my husband retires and the children get homes of their own. I'm living for that blessed day when I can get a little rest." When her husband did retire and the children were married and living in their own homes, this same mother was a very unhappy person. She looked back to the time when her husband was working and the house was full of children as the happiest period of her life.

How often we miss the joy and the happiness that is to be

found in the present because we keep thinking how much better it will be tomorrow.

"*Now* is the accepted time; *now* is the day of salvation." *Now*—not tomorrow—is the time to live. *Now*—not tomorrow—is the time to be saved, to be made whole.

Our time on earth is limited. Every moment is unique and unrepeatable. Tomorrow is not ours; today is. Now is the time to do the compassionate act. Now is the time to say the word of forgiveness—before our time runs out. Now is the most glorious period of life. God's time is always now. "Now is the accepted time."

How many good things were going to be done tomorrow, but were never done because tomorrow was always one day ahead.

Tomorrow

"He was going to be all that a mortal should be
Tomorrow.
No one would be better than he
Tomorrow.
Each morning he'd stack up the letters he'd write
Tomorrow.
It was too bad indeed he was too busy to see Bill, but he promised to do it
Tomorrow.
The greatest of workers this man would have been
Tomorrow.
The world would have known him had he ever seen
Tomorrow.
But the fact is he died and faded from view, and all that was left
when living was through
Was a mountain of things he intended to do
Tomorrow."

"Now is the accepted time; now is the day of salvation."

Remember the story of the two gamblers by Kierkegaard?

The one gambler said: "I must quit gambling. Tonight I am going to have my last fling at it, and get it out of my system, and tomorrow I will be through with it." Says Kierkegaard, "That man will never quit."

The other gambler said: "I mean to stop gambling. I cannot speak for tomorrow because tomorrow is not here yet. But as for today—as for right now—I am not gambling." Said Kierkegaard, "He will quit."

Then he goes on to say that what we are really serious about, we will do today, *now*. What we say we are serious about but are really not, we plan to do tomorrow. But as Kierkegaard pointed out, this tomorrow never arrives—only today is real. "Now is the accepted time; now is the day of salvation."

There Is No Hurry

There is an old legend according to which Satan once called a meeting of his lieutenants to seek out the best way to keep people from God. One devil said, "Let's tell them there is no God." Another said, "Let's tell them that God doesn't care about right and wrong." Finally a third one said, "Let them believe that there is a God and that He cares about right and wrong. But let's just keep whispering that *there is no hurry*." It was agreed that this last method was the best one. And Satan has been whispering in our ears ever since, "Yes, of course, you're right and you must do all these good things, but you need not do them today. There is no need to hurry. Take your time and do it when you're ready. There's always tomorrow." Thus Satan has been tempting us and keeping us from achieving most of the good things we want and intend to do. Finally, we approach the end of our lives realizing, after it is too late, that we have achieved only a tiny portion of our potential, that we have done only a small bit of the good we intended to do. We pass this way but once, and we miss most of the opportunities that present themselves to us because of tomorrow. "Now is the accepted time; now is the day of salvation."

Do It Now

I share with you these beautiful words by Phillips Brooks:

"O, my dear friends, you who are letting miserable misunderstandings run on from year to year, meaning to clear them up some day; you who are keeping wretched quarrels alive because you cannot quite make up your mind that now is the day to sacrifice your pride and kill them; you who are passing men sullenly upon the street, not speaking to them out of some silly spite, and yet knowing that it would fill you with shame and remorse if you heard that one of these men were dead tomorrow morning; you who are letting your neighbor starve, till you hear that he is dying of starvation; or letting your friend's heart ache for a word of appreciation or sympathy, which you mean to give him some day,—if only you could know and see and feel, all of a sudden, that "the time is short," how it would break the spell! How you would go instantly and do the thing which you might never have another chance to do."

What Are We Waiting For?

William Makepeace Thackeray and Charles Dickens, toward the middle of the nineteenth century, became rivals and estranged. Just before Christmas, 1863, they met in London, and frigidly failed to recognize each other. Thackeray turned back, seized the hand of Dickens and said he could no longer bear the coldness that existed between them. Dickens was touched; they parted with smiles. The old jealousy was destroyed. Almost immediately afterward Thackeray suddenly died. Sir Thomas Martin later wrote, "The next time I saw Dickens he was looking down into the grave of his great rival. He must have rejoiced, I thought, that they had shaken hands so warmly a day or so before."

"Now is the acceptable time . . . now is the time of salvation."

How often we hear people say, "I wish I had time for church, for prayer, for the Bible, for my family." We *have* time. God gives it to us. Each morning, 24 hours are presented to us. We must never be too busy to sit at the feet of Jesus to learn of Him, nor too preoccupied to go out and serve Him. There will come a time at the Judgment Seat of Christ when we shall have to give an account of what we did with all our days and hours, which can never be repeated.

Someone told of meeting a doctor friend. Seeing that the doctor was much depressed, he asked him what was the matter. The doctor replied, "I have just come from a man for whom I can do nothing. If he had come to me months ago when he first felt the twinges of the thing that will now kill him, I could have cured him quite easily. But he has let it go too far."

"Now is the accepted time . . . now is the time of salvation."

God a Stranger

Why do so many of us place God on the margin of life? Why do we forget about Him until we need Him? Is God someone of Whom we only make use? Is God a life-belt or a Friend? Surely, He should be the Friend of every step of the way, and not only the One Whom we call in an emergency. The trouble is that when we treat God so off-handedly, when the time comes that we need Him, we feel very awkward. It is as if we are addressing a stranger.

There was an old saint who spent much time in prayer. When someone asked why he prayed so much, he answered; "I talk to God every day so that when the desperate moment comes He will know my voice."

A Dangerous Word

This word "tomorrow" becomes most dangerous when it is applied to Christ and the salvation of one's soul. As a result of hearing Paul's sermon on the judgement to come, we read in the Book of Acts that Felix, the Roman governor, "trembled." He had a vision of God and the judgement to come. He was in a mood when he might have repented and turned to God. But instead he said, "Tomorrow." That tomorrow never came. Felix was never again stirred to such repentance. He died in sin and his soul was lost eternally. On his grave they placed the epitaph, Tomorrow.

PRAYER

Lord, not tomorrow but today, now. Now I come to You. Now let me express the love I may never be here to express tomorrow. Now let me believe. Now let me follow You. Now that I hear Your voice. Amen.

Temples of the Living God

Seventeenth Sunday of Matthew (2 Corinthians 6:16 to 7:1)

"For we are the temple of the living God" (2 Cor. 6:16).

If someone were to ask you, "Where does God live?" what would you answer? If you answered, "He lives in heaven," you would be right—but only partially right. The Apostle Paul tells us in today's Epistle lesson that God lives also somewhere else: "For we are the temple of the living God," he writes. It is God's fervent desire to dwell within each one of us. "Behold, I stand at the door and knock; if any one hears my voice and opens the door, I will come in to him and eat with him, and he with me" (Rev. 3:20).

The Church: God's Temple

A father brought his child to church one day and said, "This is God's house. This is where God lives." Unfortunately the father stopped at that point. He should have gone on to explain that the reason God lives in church is that He might step out of church to make His home in us. When we receive Jesus in the Sacrament of Communion, He comes to live in us. Our body becomes a chalice, a eucharistic tabernacle, a "temple of the living God."

A Kingdom Within

"The Kingdom of God is within," said Jesus. Within each one of us there is a throne. When the Lord Jesus sits on this throne; when He gives the orders and I obey, then He is King; He rules. There is a real kingdom within. If He rules, then it is the kingdom of God: a kingdom of peace and power and purpose. "For we are the temple of the living God."

There is an empty space inside that craves to be filled. There are over six million alcoholics in the United States today, sick people, primarily because their lives are empty. We take tranquilizers—hundreds of millions of prescriptions per year. We take drugs and do a thousand other things to fill the empty space within. As someone has said, "When we are not filled with the Spirit, we have to turn to spirits!"

But the empty space within was created for no one else but God. Unless He fills it, there will be boredom and unhappiness. The space within was created to be a temple for the living God, not a sewer for drugs. "For we are the temple of the living God" (2 Cor. 6:16).

The pagan Greeks looked down on the body as something evil. The body is a tomb, they said, a prison-house, a purgatory where the soul suffers to atone for its sins. Death was looked upon as a release from this prison. That God would in any sense take upon Himself a body was to the pagan Greeks incredible. Yet this is exactly what God did in Christ Jesus. He took on a human body and sanctified it, turning it into a temple, a tabernacle of God's presence. "And the Word became flesh and dwelt among us, full of grace and truth" (John 1:14).

How Marvelous the Temple

Think of how marvelous this temple—the human body—is! Take the spleen, for example. Its function is to take the million million red cells which wear out daily, reclaim the iron in them, and inject it into the bloodstream for transmission to the bone marrow, where new cells are born. Let this function fail, this tiny bit of iron be missing, and you have iron deficiency anemia.

Think of the heart—a mass of muscle, weighing about 12 ounces, which beats 100,000 times a day, exerts enough energy every 24 hours to raise a 2 pound weight 12 miles in the air, as it moves 10 tons of blood during that time through 75 to 100 thousand miles of pipes. This remarkable muscle pumps the blood through an amazing length of arteries and veins every 23 seconds, lifting 50 tones of blood between one sunrise and the next.

Think of another member of this temple of God—the human body—the brain with its 9,200,000,000 nerve cells—each single cell more complicated than the most complicated computer man can build.

No wonder Shakespeare felt compelled to cry out: "What a piece of work is man! How noble in reason! how infinite in faculty! in form and moving how express and admirable! in action how like an angel! in apprehension how like a god! the beauty of the world! the paragon of animals!"

This human body—so fearfully and wonderfully made—was created to be not a prison or a sewer—but a temple to house the living God. No other tenant has a right to live there. If he does, there will be misery, unhappiness, hell. "For we are the temple of the living God."

Give God's Temple Back to Him

When Johnny Cash was a drug addict, a jailer said to him as he released him on a drug charge: "I don't know where you think you got your talent from, Johnny, but if you think it came from God, then you're sure wrecking the body He put it in."

Finally, Johnny remembered God's word in First Corinthians 6:19, "Do you not know that your body is a temple of the Holy Spirit within you, which you have from God?

You are not your own; you were bought with a price. So glorify God in your body."

Through prayer and the power of Christ, Johnny Cash was able to lick the drug habit. He allowed Christ—the rightful tenant—to come in and expel the demons that had turned his body into a tomb.

I close with these words of Johnny Cash:

"Because of the kind of work I do, it is difficult to sweep past mistakes under the rug. Every once in a while, I meet some youngster who knows I used to be an addict, as he is now, and he asks me what he can do to kick the habit. I tell him what I learned, 'Give God's temple back to Him. The alternative is death!"

"For we are the temple of the living God" (2 Cor. 6:16).

PRAYER

Come, dear Lord, claim Your rightful place within. Sit on the throne of my heart. Let Your kingdom of peace and harmony and love become a reality within. Make me a walking temple of Your love and peace and hope wherever I go. Amen.